Amsterdam

Front cover: Amsterdam's favourite
mode of transport

Right: Traditional canalside architecture

TOP 10 ATTRACTIONS

Anne Frank House • Visit the house in which she wrote her extraordinary diary *(page 68)*

The Dam • This square is the symbolic heart of the city and home to the ornate Koninklijk Paleis *(page 64)*

Oude Kerk • Dating from the early 13th century, it is the oldest church in the city *(page 31)*

Begijnhof • Find peace and quiet in the picturesque courtyard, notable for its quaint architecture *(page 62)*

A canal cruise • A leisurely way to see the sights *(page 91)*

Van Gogh Museum • Houses a collection of hundreds of the troubled artist's works *(page 58)*

Bloemenmarkt • Colourful flowers on display all year round *(page 52)*

Hortus Botanicus • This botanical garden in the Plantage district houses more than 4,000 species of plants *(page 46)*

Rijksmuseum • Though under restoration, this is still the place to see the finest Dutch masterpieces *(page 55)*

Science Center NEMO • Get your hands on the latest science and technology in this remarkable ship-shaped museum *(page 51)*

A PERFECT DAY

9.00am Breakfast

A leisurely breakfast over the morning newspapers in a grand café, Café Luxembourg, at Spuistraat 24, should hit the spot.

12.00pm Vondelpark

Continue south to this wild and wonderful park, with its hippie-era history. There is usually plenty of free space amid the trees to escape from the city's hustle and bustle.

11.00am Leidseplein

Take a tram to Leidseplein, Amsterdam's bustling entertainment square. Maybe fit in a coffee in the spectacular Art Nouveau and Art Deco Café Americain.

1.00pm Lunch

Vondelpark has two notable eateries: Vertigo, in a 19th-century villa on the park's eastern edge, with a grand open-air terrace; and 't Blauwe Theehuis, in a contemporary round building on several levels in the park's centre, which also has outdoor tables. Either would be a good bet for lunch.

10.00am The Begijnhof

Cross over Spui to the tranquil courtyard garden of this restored medieval *hofje* (almshouse), which was once home to pious single women known as *beguines*, who carried out religious and charitable duties.

IN AMSTERDAM

4.00pm **Het IJ**

Take tram 2 or 5 from Museumplein to Centraal Station, and go to the ferry dock at the rear. Board the free Buiksloterwegveer ferry for a 5-minute trip across the IJ waterway to Amsterdam-Noord. This is a good way to get a decent view of the redeveloping harbour in a short time. Longer trips are available for those with more time.

8.00pm **Dinner**

For an indelibly Amsterdam experience, try De Prins (tel: 020-624 9382), across from the Anne Frank House on Prinsengracht. A good modern Indonesian choice is Kantjil & de Tijger, at Spui. For an after-dinner drink in a 'brown café', go to Hoppe at Spui.

2.00pm **Museum fix**

Continue to Museumplein, where you can choose between the Rijksmuseum, where the highlights of Holland's Golden Age are a wonder to behold; or the Van Gogh Museum, with the world's largest collection of Vincent's paintings.

6.00pm **Anne Frankhuis**

Board tram 13 or 17 at Centraal Station to Westerplein. Waiting times at the Anne Frank House are generally shorter in the evening. On a short visit, stick to the secret rooms where the young diarist, her family and acquaintances spent several years hiding from the Nazis.

CONTENTS

40

53

44

INTRODUCTION

There's no other city on earth like Amsterdam. It is a city of superlatives, having more canals than Venice and more bridges than Paris. It is also one of the prettiest cities in Europe. More than 50 museums – featuring everything from the world's most prominent artists to the history of cannabis – quench the thirst of even the most ardent culture buff, and with 7,000 buildings from the 16th, 17th and 18th centuries, the reflections of its illustrious past happily ripple on into the 21st century. However, the lure of Amsterdam's bricks and mortar is only part of its excitement. Its contemporary culture is vibrant – it's definitely not a city stuck in the past, and its people are open-minded, easygoing and strong-minded but also down to earth and welcoming to visitors.

Without doubt, though, a major attraction of the city is its historic buildings. The lines of tall, narrow houses with their pretty gables rest beside picture-perfect tree-lined canals. They are connected by humpback bridges and quaint cobbled walkways, which seem to have changed little in nearly 400 years – in fact, since they were walked by the artist Rembrandt and the explorer Abel Tasman, who gave his name to Tasmania.

Water world

Amsterdam contains more than 1,200 bridges crossing more than 100 canals, with a combined length of over 100km (65 miles).

Amsterdam, which lies in western Holland, close to the North Sea, is a wonderful city for visitors. It's small enough to stroll around, and, with the canalside streets too narrow for tour buses, there is no risk of sightseers driving past all the best attractions at high speed. You have to feel the sum-

Bicycles In Amsterdam are decorative as well as useful

Soaring town houses

mer sun or see your breath on a crisp winter morning to see what Amsterdam is all about. On a canal tour, the quiet boats allow you to admire the architecture from water level, floating slowly along away from the noise of the modern world.

The museums could keep you busy for weeks. Art collections, historic houses and memorials to heroes and heroines can all be found here. For entertainment after the sun sets, there are more than 40 different performances in the city every evening. The Netherlands Opera and the National Ballet are based here, and there are numerous orchestral, musical and comedy venues, along with revues and dance shows. Amsterdam also plays host to one of the most dynamic club scenes in Europe.

A Living City

The facades of the buildings may hark back to the past, but the interiors do not. Internet banking, interactive information points and recycling advice centres – the concepts of today are alive and thriving all around the city. This is no historic ghost town: the city brims with people. Its houses are still lived in (although most are now apartments rather than single-family homes), and its streets filled with bakeries, delicatessens and wine merchants where people drop in to buy dinner on the way home in the evening. It's all part of the fascinating dichotomy you find at every turn here. The city strides into the future while still holding metaphorical hands with the past.

The historic heart of Amsterdam has remained relatively unchanged mainly because of people power. In the latter part of the 20th century, as in most cities, property developers were coveting interesting locations, and in Amsterdam they had their eyes on the old canal houses, knowing they could make a tidy profit by demolishing them and replacing them with something modern. Unfashionable buildings, such as the warehouses of the old docks, were left to the elements. Some Amsterdammers, though, had other ideas. They took to the streets to fight for their city, barricading historic houses and occupying empty buildings in the warehouse district.

This was typical of the populace, and it wasn't the first time; Amsterdammers have been standing up for what they believe in for centuries. When Protestants were persecuted in the 16th century, they flocked here from all over Europe to take refuge. During World War II, the dock workers of

Barges on the Oosterdok

Amsterdam went on strike as an act of protest against the Nazis' treatment of the Jews in the city. Although in the end the protest was futile, it shows the strength of feeling and social awareness that pervades every part of society here.

Today, Amsterdam has among its population of 770,000 more than 100 different nationalities living within the city boundaries, a situation that could be fraught with difficulty and strain. Yet here it has added to the cultural richness built up over centuries of exploration and trade. That doesn't mean to say the city is free from racism, tensions between ethnic groups and concerns about immigration; all of these are perceived to have increased since the murder of film-maker Theo van Gogh by an Islamic fundamentalist in 2004.

Amsterdammers seem to have the ability to find creative solutions to their problems. When there wasn't enough housing on the land, they looked at the empty canals and decided

Illuminated bridge across the Singel canal

that houseboats would help. There are now more than 2,500 on the city's waterways. When cars became a problem in the old town they gave the bicycle priority, and now there are more than 500,000 cycles on the streets – and an estimated 30,000 at the bottom of the canal system at any one time.

Amsterdammers fight for everyone's rights against oppression, or the right of David to stand against the faceless Goliath of bureaucracy. In fact in Amsterdam when several thousand Davids get together to form a pressure group, Goliath has to sit up and take notice. Amsterdam is a city of 21st-century pressures, such as the problems of traffic and litter – but the problems are faced realistically, debated by the community,

Amsterdam 'Returns' to the Sea

After neglecting for most of the 20th century its waterfront along the channel known as Het IJ as anything other than an (admittedly vital) economic asset, Amsterdam has since been taking advantage of the ocean port's relocation to new terrain west of the city. Many of the old harbour installations – wharves, docks, dry docks, warehouses, offices, shipbuilding and ship-repair yards – have either been razed completely or converted to new purposes. Redevelopment of the harbour has afforded vast quantities of space for new housing, cultural, social, entertainment and economic projects, often in leading-edge architectural styles.

Among the highlights of this decades-long effort on the waterfront are the ultramodern Muziekgebouw aan 't IJ concert hall for contemporary music, just east of Centraal Station, and the adjacent (and equally modern) Bimhuis jazz and blues venue. Along the wharf, seagoing cruise liners berth at the Passenger Terminal Amterdam. Offshore, the connected manmade islands Java-Eiland and KNSM-Eiland have been transformed into a contemporary 'city on the water'. West of Centraal Station, it's a similar story. Take the harbour ferry to the redeveloped NDSM-Werf (NDSM Wharf), renamed the MediaWharf, a location for all kinds of creative companies.

and agreed solutions are put into action. When the solutions don't work, the process starts again. It is all seen as a huge learning curve.

Of course, Amsterdam residents don't spend all their time waving protest banners. Many are as industrious and hardworking as their forefathers. They enjoy galleries and exhibitions as much as the visitors do – it can be hard to get tickets because of local demand. And they love to socialise. Bars – particularly the 'brown bars' – are popular places in which to meet and put the world to rights. In summer, everyone drinks outside at tables in the squares and on the streets. Sit down and you may soon be engaged in conversation (most Amsterdammers speak good English).

Amsterdammers enjoy cafés

Amsterdam has many facets, yet they amalgamate into a coherent whole. It is a city of history, which shouts from every gable and corner; a city of culture – of museums, musicians and artists; a city of learning with two large universities; a city of trade with banking at its core; a multiethnic city of many different nationalities; a generally tolerant city, in which minority groups may flourish; and a city of tourism, with more than 10 million foreign visitors a year. The beauty of its buildings is undisputed, but it is the sum of all these parts that makes Amsterdam an unforgettable place to visit.

A BRIEF HISTORY

It is difficult to think of a less promising spot for what has become one of the world's major cities. Something must have been appealing about the marshy outlet of the River Amstel where it met the IJ (pronounced 'Aye'), a tidal inlet of the Zuiderzee – even though the area flooded on a regular basis with water forced in by the prevailing winter winds.

The Batavians, a Germanic tribe, travelled down the Rhine to found the first settlements in the river delta around 50BC. The land was entered on maps of the Roman Empire but, following Rome's decline, became the domain of various Germanic tribes in the Dark Ages. This probably had little effect on the settlements, whose main trade was fishing.

From Fishing to Trading

By around AD1000, the land we now call the Netherlands was ruled by a number of feudal lords, who had total power over the land and the people who lived on it. The first wooden houses were built on the site of Amsterdam in around AD1200, on artificial mounds called *terps*. The town was fortified against rival lords and against the sea water, the River Amstel being dammed at what is now the square called the Dam. This was not just to control the tides but also to manipulate trade, as it prevented seagoing ships from taking their goods up the river – they had to transfer the goods to locally owned boats for their journey. It gave the local populace a healthy income and began two important elements in the city's history: the predominance of the merchant classes and the use of barges for inland trade.

In 1275 the settlement of Amstelredamme (one of the names by which it was known) received permission from Count Floris V of Holland to transport goods on the River

Amstel without incurring tolls, giving the city a monopoly on trade along the river. In 1323 Amstelredamme became a toll-free port for beer and, once a method of preserving herring had been perfected in the late 14th century, the town also had a product with a high profit margin and began exporting fish around Europe.

The early 15th century saw a healthy expansion of trade, and the population rose dramatically. Catastrophic fires destroyed a large part of the city in 1421 and again in 1452. Following the second fire, legislation made it illegal to build with wood, and brick became the material of choice. Only a few wooden buildings remain from before the 15th-century fires. Het Houten Huys in the Begijnhof is considered to be the oldest. The legislation brought about a feast of civil engineering projects, including the building of the city wall, incorporating the Waag gate and Schreierstoren tower, in c.1480.

The Oude Kerk, Amsterdam's oldest church

The Arrival of the Spanish

Meanwhile the political climate was changing with a series of dynastic intermarriages. Philip of Burgundy began to bring some semblance of unification to the Low Countries (the region that roughly translates to the Netherlands and Belgium) in the 1420s. He was succeeded by Charles the Bold, whose daughter Maria married into the House of Habsburg. Her son Philip married Isabella of Spain and in 1500 she gave birth to Charles, the future Charles V, ruler of the Netherlands, Holy Roman Emperor, but more importantly, Charles I, king of Spain and all her dominions – an empire on which it was said the sun never set.

Spanish rule was ruthless but, for a while, Amsterdam was left alone. Its position as an important trading post kept it apart from the more barbarous behaviour in other areas. It also saw a threefold increase in its population as refugees flooded in from other parts of the empire. Diamond polishers from Antwerp and Jews from Portugal all brought their influences to the city.

Amsterdam was already developing a reputation for tolerance, as these new and disparate groups settled into the city. At the same time, Martin Luther's new Christian doctrine, Protestantism, was spreading like wildfire across Europe. The teachings of the French Protestant theologian John Calvin took a firm hold in the northern provinces of the Low Countries. It was at this time that Huguenots (French Protestants) came to Amsterdam, fleeing from persecution in their own country.

The Catholic Spanish cracked down on the heretical followers of Calvin, and in 1535 there were anti-papacy demonstrations on the Dam. Strict Catholic leaders took control of the city, and in 1567 Charles V's successor, Philip II, initiated an anti-heresy campaign: Calvinism was outlawed, and repression was ruthless.

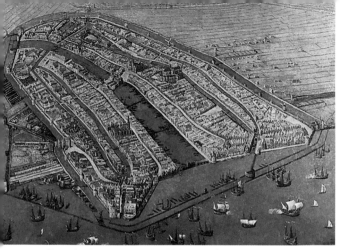

Cornelis Anthoniszoon's 1538 map of Amsterdam

Towards Independence

This atmosphere of intense fear and violence sowed the seeds of revolt. The House of Orange (with a power base around the small town of Orange in the south of France) had claim to lands in the Low Countries, and one member, William the Silent, began to organise opposition to Spanish rule. In 1578, the people of Amsterdam rose up against the papal forces and threw them from the city. Unfortunately, though, all thoughts of tolerance were forgotten and the zeal with which the Inquisition sought out Protestants was turned on Catholics. Their churches were violated, and they were forced to convert, or to worship in fearful secrecy. In 1579, seven provinces north of the Rhine concluded the Treaty of Utrecht, releasing the suffocating grip of Spanish rule. Although William was murdered in 1584, his sons continued his work, and in 1648 the treaties of The Hague and Westphalia organised the northern parts of the Low Countries into the United Provinces.

The Coming of the Golden Age

As Spanish influence faded, the Dutch star began to rise. First, they drew up agreements with the Portuguese, who had concluded trade treaties in the East that made them the sole source of goods such as spices and silks. Merchants from Amsterdam bought these goods and sold them in the north, making vast profits in the process. When the Spanish took Portugal in 1580, the Amsterdam merchants decided to go into the import business themselves, and in 1595 sent their first fleet to Asia. In 1602 the Vereenigde Oostindische Compagnie (United East India Company, or VOC) was founded in Amsterdam. It obtained a monopoly on all trade routes east of the Cape of Good Hope, founded a headquarters in Batavia (now Jakarta) in Java, and secured a monopoly trade agreement with Japan in 1641. VOC ships under the command of Abel Tasman landed in Australia some 150 years before Captain Cook.

Dutch ships brought back goods not seen before in the Western world: strange and wonderful creatures, new fruits and vegetables, and crafts of great beauty. They were all traded at immense profit with the other nations of Europe. The VOC became more powerful than many countries, Amsterdam was at the heart of this vast trading empire, and the Netherlands entered the period known as the 'Golden Age'.

Rich merchants needed banks and a financial infrastructure, and these developed quickly in the city. People flooded in to take advantage of the new com-

Dutch West Indies

The Dutch looked west as well as east, and in 1609 sent Englishman Henry Hudson from Amsterdam to search for a route to China. He traded with the native peoples of Manhattan Island (and named the Hudson River), travelled to the Caribbean, and took several islands as Dutch colonies.

mercial opportunities, the population rose rapidly, and the old medieval city simply could not cope. It was still contained within the boundaries set almost 150 years before. Plans were made for a series of three new canals – Herengracht, Keizersgracht and Prinsengracht – to form a girdle around the old medieval horseshoe. Canalside lots were sold to the wealthy, who built the finest houses they could afford, but because canal frontage was expensive, the houses were narrow and deep.

The confidence of the city brought opportunities for the burgeoning arts and sciences. The artists Rembrandt, Frans Hals, Vermeer and Paulus Potter were all working in this era, their work much in demand by the merchant classes. At the same time, the Guild of Surgeons was learning about the physiology of the body at their meeting place in the Waag, helped by Antonie van Leeuwenhoek who had invented the microscope.

Decline and Fall

During the 18th century Amsterdam grew into the world's foremost financial centre, but the seeds of decline had already been planted. When the British colonies in New Eng-

Tulip Mania

The first tulips were grown in the Netherlands in 1596 by the botanist Carolus Clusius at the botanical garden of the University of Leiden. These beautiful, colourful flowers were an instant hit – so much so that the first batch of bulbs was stolen. Early in the 17th century, as the economy experienced boom times during Amsterdam's Golden Age, wealthy merchants began to speculate in tulip bulbs, and prices for them rose to ridiculous levels. In 1637 three bulbs changed hands for a price that would have paid for a luxury canalside house. Tulipomania it was called, and it was bound to wither. When suddenly it did, not long after this high point, it drove a number of fortunes into the ground.

land rose up in revolt against the British, they found ready allies in the Dutch. From their colonies in the Caribbean they sent caches of arms and ammunition. The British were furious and went to war in 1780, destroying the Dutch Navy and precipitating a sudden decline in power and influence from which the Netherlands never recovered. Trade suffered to such an extent that in 1791 the VOC went into liquidation.

Johannes Vermeer's *Kitchen Maid* (c.1658), now in the Rijksmuseum

There were anti-Orange demonstrations by pro-French factions in the country, and in 1795 revolutionary France took the Netherlands. Under the yoke of another foreign power and with trade at an all-time low, the Golden Age was truly over.

The Return of the House of Orange

In 1806, Louis Bonaparte was installed by his brother as king of Holland and chose to make the fine Town Hall on the Dam his palace – now the Koninklijk Paleis. But Louis' secret trade links with Britain and his easygoing attitude to his subjects displeased Napoleon, and in 1810 the emperor forced his brother to abdicate and annexed his kingdom to France. When Napoleon's bubble burst and French power began to wane, William of Orange emerged from exile and was proclaimed king in 1813. Amsterdam had to work its way out of economic decline, but throughout the 19th century the city grew steadily.

WILHELM KAREL HENDRIK ERISO
PRINS VAN ORANIE EN NASSAU
ERFSTADHOUDER CAPITEIN GENERAAL
EN ADMIRAAL VAN DE SEVEN PROVINCIEN
DER VEREENIGDE NEDERLANDEN &c.& .

William of Orange

Industrialisation changed the city. With the 1889 opening of Centraal Station, built over the old harbour wall, Amsterdam turned its back on its seafaring past and looked forward towards the mechanical age. Some of the oldest canals in the city centre were filled in to allow better access to motorised vehicles. The Dam was landlocked for the first time in its history. However, in the prevailing spirit of the Victorian Age, the philanthropic city fathers funded the building of several major museums and parks, along with instigating social reforms that created what would become one of the first welfare states in the world.

The 20th Century

The Netherlands stayed neutral in World War I, and efforts in the first half of the century were concentrated on land reclamation that increased agricultural production and living space. The Zuiderzee was finally tamed with the building of a 30km (19-mile) dyke, the Afsluitdijk, in the north, creating a freshwater lake called the IJsselmeer. During the depression of the early 1930s there were several schemes designed to reduce unemployment, including the creation of the Amsterdamse Bos, a park and woodland on the outskirts of the city.

The Dutch hoped to remain neutral at the outbreak of World War II, but the Germans had other ideas and occupied the Low Countries in 1940. Amsterdammers were horrified at the treatment of their Jewish neighbours, and the dock workers staged a brave one-day strike to protest, but almost all the city's Jews were transported to concentration camps, never to return.

People Power

During the 1960s Amsterdam became a magnet for counter-culture groups such as hippies, who were drawn by the well-known open-mindedness of the people. 'People power' began to exert its influence, which ensured that, in Amsterdam at least, progress did not mean sweeping away the past. Where developers saw the opportunity to demolish derelict canal houses and warehouses, the people fought (sometimes literally) to save what they considered their heritage *(see page 11)*. Today much of the historic city is protected by statute, although any redevelopment provokes much debate. The building of the Muziektheater and Stadhuis in the 1980s, resulting in the demolition of several old houses, was a case in point, with vitriolic demonstrations by local pressure groups.

The Netherlands joined the European Union (then the European Economic Community) in 1957, seeing it as a way of increasing both their security and their economic stability. Their natural strengths in agricultural production and trade have ensured their success in the new alliance. The Amsterdam Area has become an important base for foreign companies that have trade ties in Europe. The Dutch have generally been at the forefront of the movement to open national borders, increase people's freedom of movement and expand trade within the EU. (In 2005, however, they voted against the proposed EU constitution.)

Amsterdam has become one of the premier tourist cities in the world, trading on its historic centre and its wealth of artistic collections. Today it operates much as it did in the Golden Age with banking, trade, and modern 'pilgrims' (in the form of tourists) ensuring it remains a wealthy city.

Twenty-first Century Challenges

As the second decade of the 21st century got underway, some of Amsterdam's cherished multicultural and alternative traditions faced new challenges. A small minority of poorly integrated young Muslims rejected the city's anything-goes lifestyle and engaged in sometimes violent gay-bashing and anti-Jewish activity. The situation became serious enough for the previous city mayor to ask the University of Amsterdam to study the problem and propose possible remedies. At the same time, national and city governments, responding to increasing popular pressure to combat organised crime and drugs tourism, were acting to curtail the Red Light District and the hash-smoking coffee shops. A controversial new law was floated that would permit the authorities to prevent anyone who was not a legal Dutch resident from entering the coffee shops by making them members-only clubs.

Tradition is still remembered in Amsterdam

Perhaps the only major long-term spectre, however, is the one that worried the inhabitants of Amstelredamme centuries ago: water levels. Global warming over the next few decades seemingly threatens to raise sea levels around the world, and the Netherlands – 'nether' means 'low-lying' or 'below' – will have to work hard at solving the problem for the country's future inhabitants.

Historical Landmarks

c.1200 Wooden houses built at mouth of Amstel. The river is dammed.

1275 Count Floris V of Holland grants 'Amstelredamme' the rights to carry cargoes on the river toll-free.

1300 Bishop of Utrecht grants Amsterdam its city charter.

1345 The 'Miracle of Amsterdam', basis of the Stille Omgang procession.

1419 Philip of Burgundy rises to power, unifying the Low Countries.

1452 Fire destroys wooden buildings; new ones to be of brick or stone.

1516 Spain under Charles V rules the Netherlands.

1567 Spain outlaws Calvinism: ruthless repression of Protestants.

1578 The Alteration: Protestants take control of Amsterdam.

1602 United East India Company formed, with HQ in Amsterdam.

1642 Rembrandt paints *The Night Watch*.

1600–1700 The Golden Age: a Dutch empire built on trade with the East. Canal building in Amsterdam. The arts reach a high point.

1791 The United East India Company goes into liquidation.

1795 Revolutionary France occupies the Netherlands.

1813 The House of Orange returns to power.

1889 Centraal Station opened.

1940 Neutral Netherlands invaded by German forces.

1944–5 The Winter of Hunger.

1960s 'People power' saves parts of historic Amsterdam from redevelopment. Amsterdam becomes home to minority groups.

1975 Demonstrations over plans to demolish parts of Nieuwmarkt.

1986 The 'Stopera' (Stadhuis and Opera) complex is completed.

2003 Most of Rijksmuseum closes for renovation; due to end in 2013.

2004 After making a film critical of Islam, director Theo van Gogh is murdered in Amsterdam.

2005 Muziekgebouw aan 't IJ concert hall opens on the waterfront.

2007 Council closes some prostitutes' windows in the Red Light district, to reduce organised crime and restore a measure of 'liveability'.

2010 The new national government announces its intention to ban foreign visitors from cannabis 'coffee shops'.

WHERE TO GO

Amsterdam is a small city and eminently walkable, but if you only have a short time, take advantage of the tram system, which can transport you efficiently to all the most important attractions. Perhaps the most disconcerting thing for newcomers is how to find their way around. The centre of Amsterdam can seem at first like a maze of tiny streets and canals with no overall plan. But think of it as a large spider's web, and once you understand the structure of the town, it is relatively easy to get around. The central core, around the square called the Dam, is horseshoe-shaped, and consists of a series of wide streets (the main one is Damrak/Rokin, which cuts right through the centre) and narrow alleys. It also has some of the oldest waterways, once so important for the delivery of goods from around the Dutch trading world.

I amsterdam Card

The VVV (tourist board) sells an I amsterdam Card giving free or reduced-price access to museums, canal cruises and public transport. You'll also get discounts on bike hire and even on meals at certain restaurants. A one-day card costs €39, a two-day card €49 and a three-day card €59 (2011 rates). Cards can be bought from VVV offices in Amsterdam, from Dutch tourist offices abroad or online at www.iamsterdamcard.com.

This area is ringed by a girdle of canals (*grachten*), the major ones running outward in ever larger circles. Singel was once the outer barrier for medieval Amstelredamme, but as the city expanded, Herengracht (Gentlemen's Canal), Keizersgracht (Emperor's Canal) and Prinsengracht (Princes'

Traditional canalside architecture

Just a few of Amsterdam's half a million bicycles

Canal) enlarged the web. If you ever feel confused when strolling around town, remember that these three canals spread outwards in alphabetical order: H, K and P.

Small streets *(straatjes)* radiate out from the centre, crossing the canals by means of the thousand-plus bridges, which are such a distinctive part of the city landscape. To the north of the city centre, the IJ waterway joins the IJsselmeer (a former inlet of the North Sea, now dammed); west of the IJ is the Noordzeekanaal, Amsterdam's present-day route to the open sea.

This guide divides the city into four sections that are easy to follow on foot. We start in the centre of the city, where you will be able to get your bearings, obtain whatever information you need from the VVV tourist information office *(see pages 30 and 128)* and take a **canal boat tour** – one of the best ways to get an overview of historic Amsterdam and to admire the true beauty of the city *(see page 121)*.

THE CENTRE

Central Amsterdam – once the medieval city – is very small indeed. The port was the lifeblood of the city at that time and
ships would sail right into the heart of Amstelredamme, as it
was known. Only a few architectural gems are left to remind
us of this era, but the tangle of narrow alleyways gives a feel
of the hustle and bustle that must have surrounded the traders.

Stationsplein to Damrak

The decision to locate **Centraal Station** on the site of the ◀ **①**
old harbour wall was the final death-knell of maritime trade
for the city. It stopped large cargo ships from landing their
cargoes and diminished the importance of the canal systems.

The station, opened in 1889, dominates the view up Damrak. The grand building was designed by P.J.H. Cuypers, who
was also responsible for the design of the Rijksmuseum, and
sits on three artificial islands supported by 8,687 wooden piles;
it is currently undergoing extensive restoration and expansion.

East of the station, on the newly redeveloped waterfront
north of Piet Heinkade, stands the landmark **Muziekgebouw
aan 't IJ** (literally Music Building on the IJ). It opened in
2005 and complements the classical emphasis of the better

Lean Times

As you stroll along the canalsides you will notice that there are very few
houses standing absolutely upright – in fact, some seem to lean at a pre-
carious angle. Don't assume that this is because of subsidence; most were
designed to tilt towards the canal so that goods could be winched to
the upper floors without crashing into the side of the house. Unfortunately, some of them tilted too much, resulting in the 1565 building code,
which limited the inclination to 1 in 25.

Oudezijds Voorburgwal bridge and Sint-Nicolaaskerk beyond

known Concertgebouw concert hall by focusing mainly on modern music.

Back at **Stationsplein**, in front of the station, is the **VVV Amsterdam Tourist Office** *(see page 128)*. It is housed in the Noord-Zuid Hollands Koffiehuis, dating from 1919, which was rebuilt in 1981 from the preserved pieces of the original, having been dismantled when the metro was constructed in 1972. You will also find canal tour boats moored here.

Walk across the square towards the city and, on the canal bridge, you will see on your left the distinctive spires of **Sint-Nicolaaskerk** (St Nicholas Church; www.nicolaas-paroc hie.nl; Tue–Fri 11am–4pm, Mon and Sat noon–3pm; free). This Catholic church, completed in 1887, replaced many of the secret chapels that were built for worship during the period of Catholic persecution. Once over the bridge you will be on **Damrak**. This wide boulevard was formerly a major docking area for ships from the colonies. On the left is a dock for glass-topped tour boats and beyond, at the head of Damrak, is the **Beurs van Berlage** (Berlage Stock Exchange; www.beursvanberlage.nl; generally Tue–Sun 11am–5pm, but exhibition hours vary; charge), the old stock exchange. Its refined modern lines were a revelation when it opened in 1903. Unfortunately, it didn't excite traders and is now used as a concert and exhibition hall featuring everything from chamber music to modern art.

Oude Kerk

The warren of streets to the left of the Beurs building is what Amsterdammers call the **Oude Zijde** (Old Side). This was the old warehouse district in medieval times. The narrow alleyways are darker than in the modern parts of the city and the houses are even narrower and taller. Dominating the streets is the imposing Gothic **Oude Kerk** (Old Church; www. oudekerk.nl; Mon–Sat 11am–5pm, Sun 1–5pm; tower: Sat–Sun 1–5pm; charge). ◀ ③

The Oude Kerk is the oldest parish church in Amsterdam; work began in the early 13th century when Amstelredamme was a new trading town. Over the next three centuries, the church underwent several extensions until it took on the unusual shape it has today, with several chapels adding gables to the original structure. In the early days it acted as a marketplace and a hostel for the poor.

The stained-glass windows of the Oude Kerk

The Red Light District is one of the liveliest areas after dark

Inside, the scale of the church is impressive. Commemorative tombstones, including that of Saskia, Rembrandt's wife, cover the floor. The stained-glass windows are glorious. One, commemorating the Peace of Münster, shows a Spanish official handing over the charter recognising the independent Dutch state. Opposite the Oude Kerk, is a step-gabled, Baroque Dutch Renaissance house, **De Gecroonde Raep** (The Crowned Turnip), dating from 1615.

The Red Light District

The northern reaches of the canalside streets Oudezijds Voorburgwal and Oudezijds Achterburgwal, southwest of the Oude Kerk, are home to Amsterdam's infamous **Red Light District**, known as the Wallen (Walls), or the Walletjes (Little walls). As in any large port, prostitution has always been rife and, although some Calvinists tried to stamp it out, it still thrives today. In modern Amsterdam the industry has been legitimised and regulated in an attempt to curb the most disturbing facets of exploitation and to address health concerns. Prostitutes in the Netherlands are entitled to regular health checks and are expected to pay taxes on their earnings – a typically pragmatic Dutch solution to a social issue.

The area is safe (except perhaps in the early hours of the morning) and usually busy with tourists. The tree-lined canals and old, narrow iron bridges are some of the prettiest in the city, and most prostitutes ply their trade behind relatively discreet windows, not on the streets.

At ground level, there are shops – seedy, eye-catching or amusing, depending on your point of view – selling sex wares and attracting customers. But don't get too distracted, or you will miss the rows of dainty gables, quirky wall plaques and window boxes brimming with flowers, which give the whole area a cheery feel. Don't be surprised to find offices, shops and restaurants side by side with the brothels here – it's all part of Amsterdam life. At night the streets come alive with bars, clubs and adult shows and it becomes one of the liveliest parts of the city. Make sure you stay on the busier, well-lit thoroughfares on your way back to your hotel.

Sex and Drugs

Perhaps Amsterdam's most widely publicised acts of tolerance in recent history have been in the areas of the sex industry and drug taking. Amsterdammers have looked at feasible and practical responses to the issues, and decriminalised some aspects of both. This does not make the city one big den of iniquity, and these areas are still controlled and regulated; in fact, you could visit Amsterdam and be quite unaware of these activities. There is just a recognition here that, provided no harm comes to you or others around you, then you should be free, as an adult, to make your own choices.

Museum Het Amstelkring

You will find several historical gems as you wander the Wallen. One of the narrow houses on Oudezijds Voorburgwal (No. 40) has a wonderful secret to share. **Ons' Lieve Heer op Solder** (Our Lord in the Attic; www.opsolder.nl; Mon–Sat 10am–5pm, Sun and holidays 1–5pm; charge) was a merchant's house bought by the Catholic Jan Hartman in 1661. Following the 'Alteration' in 1578, Catholics were not permitted to practise their religion, so Hartman, along with a number of other wealthy Catholics of the time, had a secret chapel built for family worship. Although they were common at the time, this is now the only complete secret chapel left in the city. Three additional houses were added to create extra space, and several of the other rooms are furnished in 18th-century style. It is a fascinating glimpse of a difficult time in Amsterdam's history, but it's not just a museum piece – it is still used for weddings.

De Waag is one of the city's oldest buildings

A few doors along from the Amstelkring is the Dutch Renaissance **D'Leeuwenburg Huis**, a restored step-gabled house dating from 1605.

De Waag

Southeast of the Oude Kerk you can walk through the small Chinese Quarter to reach **De Waag** (Weigh House). One of the oldest buildings in the city, it opened in 1488 as a city gate to mark the eastern boundary of the city along the new wall built after the disastrous

Stopping for a rest at Nieuwmarkt

fire in the 1450s. The numerous turrets and rounded tower give it the look of a fairy-tale castle but it has had a more gruesome history. Public executions were held here in the 16th century, with the condemned being kept in a small cell on the ground floor before they met their fate.

From the early 17th century it became the weigh house *(waaggebouw)* for cargoes entering or leaving the city down the Geldersekade canal to the north. The upper floors were used by trades' guilds for meetings and by the Guild of Surgeons for practical medical research, including experiments with cadavers. Two of Rembrandt's most celebrated paintings, *The Anatomy Lesson of Dr Deijman* and *The Anatomy Lesson of Dr Tulp* were commissioned by the Guild of Surgeons and originally hung in the Waag.

In the early 19th century the weigh house closed, and the Waag had a number of less illustrious tenants. It now houses a superb café-restaurant, called In de Waag *(see page 106)*, so

The Schreierstoren

you can stop for refreshment and admire the Gothic interior at the same time.

Nieuwmarkt and Zuiderkerk

Nieuwmarkt (New Market) surrounds the Waag and is home to several different types of market throughout the week (there's an organic produce market on Saturday). If you walk to the north side of the Waag and look along Geldersekade you will see a tower dominating the skyline. This is the **Schreierstoren**, which is also part of the new city wall that was constructed in 1480. City historians are divided as to the reason for the tower's name. Some say it comes from the word *schreien*, which means 'weeping', as it was a place where sailors' wives came to wave their men off to sea, fearing for their safety. However, others claim that the name is a derivation of the word *scherpe* (sharp), describing the tower's position on a 90-degree bend in the wall. The tower now houses the VOC Café, an attractive old-style bar.

From the Waag walk down Sint-Antoniesbreestraat, past modern apartment blocks built in the 1970s. Look out for the magnificent **De Pintohuis** at No. 69, a mansion bought by wealthy Jewish merchant Isaäc de Pinto in 1651, and rebuilt in 1686 by his son David Emanuel, who gave it more or less its present ornate appearance.

Off the right side of Sint-Antoniesbreestraat is the ornate tower of the **Zuiderkerk** (South Church; Mon–Fri 9am–5pm, Sat noon–4pm; free; tower: Apr–Sept Tue–Sun 1–5pm; charge). Begun in 1603, this was the city's first Protestant place of worship to be built after the Reformation. Designed by Hendrick de Keyser, it was deconsecrated in 1929 and is now the (probably temporary) location of the provisional **Nationaal Historisch Museum** (National Historical Museum; www.innl.nl), a footloose institution that is seeking both a home and funding to get off the ground.

At the end of Sint-Antoniesbreestraat is a tiny square with a wonderful view along Oude Schans to your left. You will find an old house, now a small bar/café, De Sluyswacht, in the foreground and the **Montelbaanstoren** behind. Built as part of a new outer defensive wall in 1512, the tower originally had a flat roof – the ornate peak that gives it such panache was added by Hendrick de Keyser in 1606. Today it is used by a Dutch foundation, the Stichting Secret Garden (ww.stichtingsecretgarden.nl), which represents LGBT (lesbian, gay, bisexual and transgender) Muslims.

Rembrandt's Inspiration

Rembrandt van Rijn had a passion for collecting rare or precious objects. This desire played a part in his downfall, but his collection at the Rembrandthuis (see page 38) tells us much about Dutch society in the 1600s. Beautiful man-made items from the Dutch colonies sit beside Roman and Greek sculptures from the Classical era. There are a number of globes, indicating the expansion of the known world in Rembrandt's time, seashells and strange stuffed beasts from far-off lands, and etchings by Raphael, Titian and Holbein, kept in heavy leather-bound books, showing new visual styles in form and colour. Inspiration was rich indeed in 17th-century Amsterdam.

The Polders

Some 6,500 sq km (2,500 sq miles) of the Netherlands has been reclaimed from the sea. This was achieved by building dykes along the coast, rivers and canals, and pumping the ground water to the far side of the dyke to dry out the land. The reclaimed tracts of land between the dykes are called polders. Many areas of Amsterdam, such as Vondelpark, are 2m (6.7ft) below sea level, and Schiphol Airport is 4.5m (15ft) below sea level.

Rembrandt's House

After pausing to take a photo, cross the street to Jodenbreestraat (Jewish Broad Street) and the three-storey brick building with red shutters. This is the **Museum Het Rembrandthuis** (Rembrandt House Museum; www.rembrandthuis.nl; daily 10am–5pm; charge, tickets can be purchased online), which was home to the great artist from 1639 to 1660. Rembrandt bought the house as he rose in prestige and wealth. He created a studio on the top floor, where there was abundant natural light to illuminate his subjects, and sufficient space for him to teach his numerous pupils. The painter lived with his wife, Saskia, and their young son on the first floor. Unfortunately, he was not able to live out his life in his home. His lack of financial acumen and love of expensive objects brought him to bankruptcy in 1656 and he had to sell all his possessions, including the house, in 1660.

The whole house was restored in the late 1990s, including the studio and the painter's *kunstkamer* or art cabinet *(see page 37)*, to re-create the early 1600s as faithfully as possible. The artist's studio, north facing and flooded with light, is wonderfully atmospheric, and the kitchen, with its open fireplace, is always popular with visitors. More than 250 of the artist's etchings are beautifully presented around the upper floors of the house.

THE SOUTHEAST

Waterlooplein

Parallel to Jodenbreestraat, on its left-hand side, is **Waterlooplein**, named after the famous battle and home to a flea market of the same name. Every day (except Sunday) you'll find an eclectic mix of second-hand crockery, clothing and electricals on sale, along with cotton clothes from India or Indonesia.

The eastern end of the market square is dominated by the twin spires of **Mozes en Aäronkerk** (Moses and Aaron Church), a Catholic church built in 1840 on the site of a secret chapel. The Old Testament figures of Moses and Aaron were found depicted on gable stones in the original building and were set into the wall of the new edifice. The fine towers are actually wood rather than stone. They were painted to match the sandstone walls in a 1990 restoration.

The flea market at Waterlooplein is the oldest in Amsterdam

The picturesque Magere Brug

Waterlooplein, and its market, used to be much larger, but a massive building project, begun in the early 1980s, reduced its size considerably. Protesters deplored the loss of several old canal houses fringing the square, which constituted much of what was left of the old Jewish Quarter. In the 1980s squatters battled against riot police and water cannons. Nevertheless, the construction went ahead, and the result of this labour is the conjoined **Muziektheater** (www.hetmuziektheater.nl) and **Stadhuis** (Town Hall), sitting majestically on the River Amstel. Opened in 1986, the attractive glass-fronted Muziektheater is home to the Netherlands Opera and the National Ballet and hosts a range of travelling companies in the largest auditorium in the country.

At one end of Waterlooplein is the **Joods Verzetmonument**, a black marble memorial commemorating Jewish Resistance fighters from World War II.

Towards Magere Brug

The **River Amstel** has always been a major artery through the city and even today you will see a large amount of commercial traffic passing along the waterway. From the terrace and walkway around the Muziektheater there are wonder-

ful views of the boats and the canal houses bordering the
water. The bridge in front of the Muziektheater provides a
wonderful view down the river and is also one of the most
interesting bridges in Amsterdam. The **Blauwbrug** (Blue
Bridge) is named after the colour of the previous bridge that
occupied the site. The present one, dating from 1880, is
based on Pont Alexandre III in Paris and is ornamented with
carvings of ships and other maritime themes.

A block upstream from the Blauwbrug on the east (right)
bank is the neoclassical Amstelhof (1681), a former nursing
home that is now the site of the **Hermitage Amsterdam** ◀ **9**
(www.hermitage.nl; daily 10am–5pm, Wed until 8pm; charge),
a branch of St Petersburg's State Hermitage Museum.

Although the Blauwbrug is the most ornate bridge in the
city, Amsterdammers and visitors alike have a soft spot for
its neighbour a little way south up the Amstel, the **Magere
Brug** or 'Skinny Bridge'. This white, wooden drawbridge is
picture-perfect and one of the most enduring symbols of the
city. It is even prettier at dusk when the lights on its arches
and spars are switched on. There has been a bridge here since
the 1670s but the present one was erected only in 1969.

Along the river on either side of the Magere Brug are a number of old barges moored along the banks. The large craft,

The Skinny Sisters

How did the Magere Brug get its name? *Mager* means 'skinny' in Dutch,
and it would be simple to assume that its name refers to the narrow-
ness of the bridge. Not so, say Amsterdammers, who will regale you with
stories of two sisters called Mager who each had a house on opposite
sides of the bridge and who paid for the original bridge to be built. By
amazing coincidence, these two sisters were also thin, which prompts
comments about the 'mager Mager sisters'

which would once have carried heavy cargoes such as grain and coal, now make surprisingly large, comfortable, quirky and very expensive homes. Beyond, on the east bank of the Amstel, you will see the facade of the **Koninklijk Theater Carré** (www.theatercarre.nl). Traditionally the site of the Carré Circus, this was where the Carré family had a wooden building erected to house their shows. Later the authorities deemed this structure to be a fire hazard and so the Carrés had this beautiful stone building designed for them. It opened for performances in 1887 and now hosts many different types of performance throughout the year, but a circus always appears here at Christmas time.

Herengracht
Cross the river via the Magere Brug then travel one block north and take a left along the northern bank of **Heren-**

The Golden Age kitchen in the Museum Willet-Holthuysen

gracht. Here, you will get your first look at the canal system that was built during Amsterdam's 17th-century Golden Age, revolutionising the city. During its time, this was probably the most sought-after, expensive real estate in the world.

Herengracht has numerous beautiful houses, which can only really be appreciated by strolling past them. This part of town is still mostly residential, and many houses have been converted into apartments for wealthy and successful Amsterdammers. It is fascinating to peek inside at the ultramodern interiors, which give a feel of the flair the Dutch have for interior design.

Museum Willet-Holthuysen

At No. 605 Herengracht, the **Museum Willet-Holthuysen** ◀ 🔟 (www.willetholthuysen.nl; Mon–Fri 10am–5pm, Sat–Sun and holidays 11am–5pm; charge) gives you the opportunity to look behind the facade of a genuine Golden Age house. It was completed in 1687 and structurally has changed very little since that time, although it has been altered cosmetically several times as fashions changed.

In 1855 it came into the possession of the Holthuysen family. Gerard Holthuysen was a successful trader in glass and English coal. After the death of Gerard and his wife, the house was inherited by their daughter Louisa, who later married Abraham Willet. He had a love of art and was a founding member of the Dutch Royal Antiquarian Society, whose aim was to promote national art and history.

On her death in 1895, Louisa bequeathed the house and its contents to the city of Amsterdam on the one condition

An opulent bed at
the Museum Van Loon

that it would be opened as a museum. This it duly was in 1896, and today visitors can examine in detail the furniture, porcelain and numerous artworks that had been collected by the Willet-Holthuysen family over many years.

Museum Van Loon and Reguliersgracht

Continue south a short distance towards Keizersgracht where at No. 672 you will find a canalside residence dating from 1672 that houses the **Museum Van Loon** (Wed–Mon 11am–5pm; charge; www.museum vanloon.nl). Its elegant interior includes portraits from generations of the influential Van Loon family and, in the ornamental garden, there is a coach house in the style of a Greek temple.

Travel further along Herengracht to the end of the second block. Here you will find one of the most fascinating views of the canal ring. From the bridge at **Reguliersgracht** it is possible to see 14 other bridges by looking up and down Herengracht and ahead down adjoining Reguliersgracht (this view is even better at water level, so take a canal cruise – and your camera – *see page 121*). Reguliersgracht has some very pretty houses and is quieter than the main three 'girdle' canals which were built at the same time.

Thorbeckeplein and Rembrandtplein

The small square here is **Thorbeckeplein**, where you will see a sombre statue of Johan Rudolf Thorbecke who designed the Dutch Constitution in 1848. Wander through the square, which is the scene of an art market on Sunday, to reach **Rembrandtplein**, one of the city's most vibrant social centres. This square was formerly called Botermarkt (a butter market was held here in the 19th century) but it was renamed when the large statue of Rembrandt was sited here in 1878.

One wonders what the artist would have made of the square, since it is now busy with theatres, cinemas, clubs, show halls, bars and restaurants – and dominated by vibrant neon signs. On a summer evening, however, it is a wonderful place to sit with a drink and watch the world go by. In 2009 the square's layout was reorganised, giving it a more open character.

The Jewish Quarter

Beyond the eastern end of Waterlooplein you will see the Mr Visserplein, busy with several lanes of traffic. Head across the square to Weesperstraat and Jonas Daniël Meijerplein to find the **Joods Historisch Museum** (Jewish Historical Museum; www.jhm.nl; daily 11am–5pm; charge), which documents the history of the once large and influential Jewish community in the city. Jewish history in Amsterdam dates back to the late 16th century, but was cut short by the Nazi occupation of the city that began in 1940.

Explore Jewish culture at the Joods Historisch Museum

The 17th-century
Portugese Synagoge

The systematic deportation of the Jewish population to concentration camps tore the community apart, and after the war only a handful returned to their homes. The museum, which opened in 1987, was created by the amalgamation of four old Ashkenazi synagogue buildings. The exhibitions reveal the history of Amsterdam's Jewish community, explain the philosophies of Judaism and examine the wider issues of Jewish identity.

Across busy Weesperstraat are two other reminders of the once thriving Jewish community. In a stark, exposed position near the road in Jonas Daniël Meijerplein, is the **Dokwerker Statue** by Mari Andriessen. This figure commemorates the day in February 1941 when the dock workers rose up in protest against the Nazi deportation of the Jews. Behind the statue is the **Portugese Synagoge** (www.esnoga.com; Apr–Oct Sun–Fri 10am–4pm, Nov–Mar Sun–Thur 10am–4pm, Fri 10am–2pm; charge), inaugurated in 1675 for the Spanish and Portuguese Sephardic Jews who settled in the city. Its design is said to be based on that of King Solomon's Temple.

The Plantage

From Jonas Daniël Meijerplein look southeast to the glass houses of the **Hortus Botanicus** (Botanical Garden; www.dehortus.nl; July–Aug Mon–Fri 9am–9pm, Sat–Sun 10am–9pm, Feb–June and Sept–Nov Mon–Fri 9am–5pm, Sat–Sun 10am–5pm, Dec–Jan daily until 4pm; charge), easily seen just across Nieuwe Herengracht. Cross the canal by walking left along its banks to the nearby bridge. Once across, you have entered the Plantage area of the city, formerly an area of parkland but developed from the mid-19th century into one of the first of Amsterdam's suburbs.

The Botanical Garden has a long and illustrious history. It began as a small medicinal garden in 1682, but soon became the depository for many of the new plant species brought from Dutch colonies in the Golden Age, and was responsible for developing each genus for cultivation, propagation and commercial exploitation. The distinctive glass houses were added in 1912, and today the gardens have one of the largest collections in the world.

A two-minute walk down Plantage Middenlaan leads you to **Artis** (www.artis.nl; May–Oct Sun–Fri 9am–6pm, Sat until ◀ **16** sunset, Nov–Apr daily 9am–5pm; charge), a fascinating complex of zoo, aquarium, planetarium and geological museum,

Exploring the Hortus Botanicus

Exhibits in the Tropenmuseum

which aims to increase visitors' knowledge of the physical world. The zoo was one of the first in Europe when it opened its doors in 1838, and it has continued as a ground-breaking institution, now acting as a centre for efforts to save several endangered species. Many of the old, confined Victorian enclosures where specimens were kept, were redeveloped in the 1990s to create a more pleasant environment for the animals. The **Planetarium** and other areas of Artis offer many fun ways to learn about the world around us.

Tropenmuseum

Southeast of Artis, across two canals and busy roads, is **Oosterpark**, an open green area with a lake and play areas (take tram No. 9 or 14 rather than walking here from the city centre). In the northern corner of the park is the **Tropenmuseum** (Tropical Museum: www. tropenmuseum.nl; daily 10am–5pm; charge), once the home of the Dutch Colonial

Institute. The building was constructed in 1926 to house the institute's collection of artefacts from the tropics. Today, the aim of the museum is to improve our knowledge of the world's tropical areas and promote an understanding of the peoples in these developing parts of the world. A vast collection of artefacts from the former Dutch East Indies (now Indonesia) was the starting point for the displays, which range from tribal masks to tools and utensils. Recreations of a Bombay street and Arab souk, among other locales, bring home the reality of life in different societies. The museum also has a **Tropenmuseum Junior** (Children's Museum) offering 6- to 13-year-olds a chance to explore the collection and interact with the exhibits. Special guides show children the artefacts and explain their context.

Entrepotdok

North of Artis is **Entrepotdok**, which, in the 19th century, was the warehouse region of the city with carefully designed canals forming one of the busiest port areas in Europe. The warehouses fell into disrepair in the 20th century and lay empty for many years before they became a centre for the 1960s' and 1970s' squatter revolution that overtook the city. Since the 1980s, the area has been totally renovated and the

Amsterdam Street Addresses

A formal system of addresses with street names and numbers was only introduced to the city by the French in 1795. Before this, gable stones and wall plaques were used as a way of indicating either the purpose of a commercial building or of explaining the precise site of a home. Directions might have been something like 'three doors down from the Red Fox'. Some of these plaques have been left in place – look out for them as you stroll the banks of the canals warehouses gutted to create spacious modern housing, offices, and bars and restaurants without changing the basic design of the buildings.

Heading north, you will reach the main street, Prins Hendrikkade, which takes you back to Centraal Station, to the left. As you cross over the Nieuwe Vaart canal, look left for a glimpse of the only windmill left in the city's central area. The **De Gooyer windmill** was built in the early 18th century to grind corn. It now houses a small brewery, Brouwerij 't IJ, and a bar.

The Scheepvaartmuseum

Across the bridge, walk towards Kattenburgerplein and a large square building housing the **Scheepvaartmuseum** (Maritime Museum; www.scheepvaartmuseum.nl; due to reopen in September 2011 after extensive renovation). A replica sailing ship will once again be docked outside when renovation is complete. This building was constructed in 1656 for the Navy, and its strong walls safeguarded a vast arsenal that once protected Dutch interests around the world. Extensive exhibits document the long, illustrious history of maritime achievement of the Dutch, with paintings, maps and maritime models explaining the part that ships – and particularly those of the United East India Company – played in the growth of the empire in the 17th century.

Science Center NEMO

Next to the museum, and recognisable by its vast bulk and huge green outer walls, is the **Science Center NEMO** (www.e-nemo.nl; Tue–Sun 10am–5pm, daily 9am–6pm in school holidays; charge). Designed by architect Renzo Piano, and opened in 1997, the centre was created to bring the latest science and technology into the hands of visitors, whatever their age.

A life-size replica of the *Amsterdam*

The location of the NEMO itself is a technological marvel. It sits high above the entrance to the IJ tunnel, which takes six lanes of traffic under the IJ waterway to Amsterdam's northern suburbs and beyond. Inside the centre you can try your hand at playing the stock exchange by computer, change the wheel on a car, or look at the cells of the body through a microscope. There are hands-on experiments for everyone from young children to adults, focusing on five linked themes: Energy, Humanity, Interactivity, Science and Technology.

Outside the museum is the re-creation of the United East India Company ship **Amsterdam**, a life-size replica of a real ship, completed in 1748. The ship is temporarily moored here while the Scheepvaartmuseum is under restoration. The *Amsterdam* has a crew to man her. As you explore her decks, the captain will illustrate his course with charts of the time, the doctor will explain his rather primitive treatments, and ordinary seamen will be happy to sing you a Dutch sea shanty.

THE SOUTHWEST

The southwest section takes on a fan shape from the centre of the city, widening as it travels out and encompassing the major art museums.

Muntplein

Our starting point is **Muntplein**, at the junction of the River Amstel and the Singel canal. Although only a small square, and cut by numerous tramlines, it has a particularly beautiful tower **20** – **Munttoren** (Mint Tower), originally a medieval gate guarding the entrance to the city. It was damaged by fire in 1619, and the clock tower was added by Hendrick de Keyser during the renovations. In 1699 the carillon was installed, and this still fills the air with its tinkling sounds. During the war with France in 1672, when Amsterdam's supply of money was cut off, the tower became the city mint, and the name has stuck. Just along the canal is the gruesome **Torture Museum** (www.torturemuseum.com; daily 10am–11pm; charge).

Fresh flowers for sale at the Bloemenmarkt

Bloemenmarkt

In the shadow of the tower and partly floating on the Singel (the medieval protective moat for the city) is

21 ► the **Bloemenmarkt** (Flower Market). The daily market has been held for centuries, when the flower sellers would arrive by canal with boats laden with blooms. Today the stalls still float on barges permanently attached to the canal wall. The blooms they sell bring a splash of colour to even the dullest Amsterdam day.

Café culture at Leidseplein

Stroll along the market until you reach Koningsplein and turn left down Leidsestraat. This major shopping street is always busy because it links one of the largest squares in the city to the central area. Stop at Metz&Co department store, which sits on the corner of Keizersgracht and Leidsegracht. One of the oldest shops in Amsterdam, it offers good views of the city from the café on the top floor.

Leidseplein

At the end of Leidsestraat is **Leidseplein**, the busiest square **22** in the city, with bars and cafés spilling onto it; it's a major nightlife focus, too. Look out for a small grassy area, with sculptures of life-size iguanas and other large lizards. The narrow streets leading off the square are full of cinemas, concert halls and intimate live venues.

In summer you will find several different street performers vying for your euros. It's a place where talented music students play classical pieces, or musicians from around the world play their traditional tunes, taking their turn with jugglers, mime artists and magicians. Whatever the time of year, as the sun sets, the neon lights are switched on, and people flock to enjoy the restaurants and nightclubs that keep the square buzzing until the early hours of the morning.

On the western side of Leidseplein you will find the **Stadsschouwburg** (Municipal Theatre), built in 1894. Once the premier opera house in the city, it has been usurped by the Muziektheater, but still hosts regular performances of visiting and Dutch theatre companies, being home to the Toneelgroep drama group. Across the square is the **American Hotel**, an Art Nouveau treasure and national monument completed in 1902. Non-residents can visit the Café Americain on the ground floor to enjoy the sumptuous surroundings.

Vondelpark

Turn left after Leidseplein and across the Singel you will find the **Holland Casino Amsterdam** and the **Lido Club** on your left. On your right, across Stadhouderskade, is a narrow gate into **Vondelpark**, a park that has been called 'the lungs of Amsterdam'. It was founded in 1865 after a number of philanthropic city fathers decided there was a need for a genteel recreation area for the city's population, many of whom lived in overcrowded slums. The park was named after the Netherlands' premier poet and playwright Joost van den Vondel and designed in the English fashion of the times. It originally served as a private park, paid for by the wealthy families who lived around it. Today its 46 hectares (120 acres) have farm animals, flocks of parakeets, jogging tracks and cycle paths.

The large pavilion, which opened in 1881, is now the **EYE Film Instituut Nederland** (www.filmmuseum.nl; Mon–Fri 9am–10pm, Sat–Sun 4 or 5–10.15pm; charge for screenings) which is due to move to a new building on the north bank of the IJ waterway in Amsterdam-Noord at the end of 2011. It shows more than 1,000 films each year, including outdoor screenings.

Museumplein

Only five minutes to the south of Leidseplein is the Museum Quarter, for many visitors the main reason for their visit to Amsterdam. Here, three of the most important art collections in Europe normally sit side by side, allowing visitors to walk from one to the next in a matter of moments. Although all very different in appearance, they are brought together by an open space which in the late 1990s was redesigned and replanted to accentuate the buildings. The square is called, not surprisingly, **Museumplein**.

Rijksmuseum

The highlight of any art lover's trip to Amsterdam is the **Rijksmuseum** (State Museum; www.rijksmuseum.nl; daily 9am–6pm; charge), which is home to arguably the greatest collection of Dutch art in the world. However, most of the

Vondelpark, 'the lungs of Amsterdam'

museum has been closed for renovation for several years, with the work due to continue until 2013. Fortunately, one section, the Philips Wing, remains open for the display of key works in the collection, under the title 'Rijksmuseum: The Masterpieces' some of which are detailed below. To check on progress and to find out what is on show, visit the museum's website *(see above)*.

The Rijksmuseum is housed within a magnificent Victorian Gothic building, designed by P.J.H. Cuypers and opened in 1885. Additions were completed in 1898 and 1919. The collection is varied, but most visitors come to see the works of the Dutch masters from the 15th to the 17th centuries. Among the collection are 20 works by Rembrandt, including *The Night Watch*, properly entitled *The Company of Captain Frans Banning Cocq and Lieutenant Willem van Ruytenburch*. The work, which was commissioned by the company for its barracks, is remarkable for its lack of formality and very different from the accepted style of the day. Its size is impressive, yet it was originally even larger. It was moved to the Town Hall in 1715 but was too wide for the place that had been chosen to display it, so the canvas was trimmed to make it fit, totally removing three figures on the right side of the painting. Originally, the picture showed the two major subjects towards the left of the scene. Now they stand in the centre, altering for ever the original focus of Rembrandt's composition.

Self-portrait of Rembrandt, painted in 1669

Johannes Vermeer is well represented, and his effective

Rembrandt's *The Night Watch*

use of light can be seen in *The Kitchen Maid*, painted *c*.1658–60 and now one of the gallery's best-loved pieces. There are paintings by Frans Hals, the founding artist of the Dutch School, along with a collection of Dutch artists who were influenced or schooled by the masters. Rembrandt was a prolific teacher and his pupils produced work so similar to his that many were mistaken for the great artist's work.

Look out also for the painting by a lesser-known artist, Gerrit Adriaensz Berckheyde, of Herengracht in 1672 when its grand houses were being completed. The scene has no trees and shows the 'Gentlemen's Canal' in pristine condition.

Later works include a number by Dutch artists of the Hague School, which flourished in the late 1800s and whose best-known representative is Jan van Huysum. The museum also has a collection of work by non-Dutch artists, including Rubens, Tintoretto and El Greco, along with porcelain, furniture, sculpture and decorative arts, and Asiatic art.

Amsterdam's strikingly modern
Van Gogh Museum

Van Gogh Museum

Visible just behind the Rijks-museum are the modern lines of the **Van Gogh Museum** ◄ 25 (www.vangoghmuseum.nl; daily 10am–6pm, Fri until 10pm; charge), devoted to the work of the Dutch master. The main building, by Gerrit Rietveld, opened in 1973; a separate circular wing, by Kisho Kurokawa, hosts temporary exhibitions. The museum houses more than 200 paintings and 500 drawings by the painter, covering all periods of his troubled career. The bulk of the collection was collated by Vincent's brother Theo van Gogh, who also kept more than 800 letters written by his brother.

Vincent's working life was short but frenetic, interspersed with periods of manic depression, and his paintings reflect his moods. His 1885 work *The Potato Eaters* shows the hard lives endured by the rural poor among whom he lived at this time. Contrast this with the superb vibrant colours of *The Bedroom in Arles* and *Vase with Sunflowers*, both painted after Vincent moved to Provence in 1888.

Stedelijk Museum and Surrounding Area

Next door to the Van Gogh Museum is the city's modern art 26 ► collection, the stately **Stedelijk Museum** (Municipal Museum; www.stedelijk.nl; due to reopen at the end of 2011 after a lengthy period of renovation and extension; charge). The famous 1895 facade is neoclassical, with figures such as the architect and sculptor Hendrick de Keyser (1565–1621) gazing down on the passing crowds. It was built specifically to house the private art collection of Sophia de Bruyn, who then bequeathed it to the city in 1890. In 1938 it became the museum of modern art. The museum's permanent collection includes pieces by Marc Chagall, Picasso, Monet, Cézanne and Matisse. There is also a comprehensive examination of the art

Dutch Masters Old and New

The Golden Age of the Netherlands (roughly speaking, the 17th century) produced a number of brilliant artists who left a rich legacy of work. In the years since, there have been further shining lights.

Frans Hals (c.1580–1666) is considered the founder of the Dutch School of realistic painting. He introduced to fine art the captured moment – the glance or casual expression not formerly seen in formal portraits. His celebrated portrait *The Laughing Cavalier* is in the Rijksmuseum.

Rembrandt Harmenszoon van Rijn (1606–69). Today, the best known artist of the Dutch School, Rembrandt revolutionised painting with his informal composition and use of light. He lived in Amsterdam for much of his life. Some of his best work is in the Rijksmuseum and a collection of his sketches at his house (Museum Het Rembrandthuis).

Johannes (Jan) Vermeer (1632–75) painted only around 30 works, but his attention to detail and sympathetic use of light later made his work famous. His *The Kitchen Maid* is in the Rijksmuseum.

Jacob van Ruisdael (c.1628–82). Master of the landscape, he had the ability to create an almost photographic realism. A number of his works are in the Rijksmuseum.

Vincent van Gogh (1853–90) developed his strong use of form and colour after he settled in Provence. Suffering from mental illness, he died after shooting himself just before his revolutionary work was recognised. The Van Gogh Museum has more than 200 of his paintings.

Piet Mondrian (1872–1944) brought painting down to its essence, with stark abstract lines and blocks created using primary colours. Examples of his work can be viewed at the Stedelijk Museum.

and design movement known as De Stijl (The Style), which swept through the Netherlands just after World War I.

Diamond Territory

If you feel culturally exhausted after your 'museum-fest', the streets around Museumplein offer some exciting retail therapy. Walk across Paulus Potterstraat from the Van Gogh Museum and you will find **Coster Diamonds**, one of the oldest 'houses' in the city, where you can watch diamonds being polished and maybe buy a carat or two. Van Baerlestraat, bordering the west side of Museumplein, is the haute couture area of the city. For culture of a musical nature go to the

Concertgebouw on Van Baerlstraat, home to the orchestra of the same name. The main auditorium is considered to have almost perfect acoustics, even though the designer of the building, Adolf Leonard van Gendt, had no experience in this specialised area.

Nieuwe Spiegelstraat and the Golden Bend

If you want to stroll back to town after your visit to the museums, then walk through the open courtyard that cuts through the centre of the Rijksmuseum, across Stadhouderskade and on to narrow Spiegelgracht and its continuation **Nieuwe Spiegelstraat**. This centre of antiques and art galleries has some wonderful windows to gaze into. Prices tend to be high, but the dealers are some of the most experienced in the world and they are sure to give you good advice.

Walk north along the length of Nieuwe Spiegelstraat and you will eventually reach Herengracht at its most spectacular point. When it was first dug, and the lots of land sold, it was soon realised that this section of the canal (between Vijzelstraat and Leidsestraat) would have the largest houses inhabited by the richest families in the city. For this reason it has become known as the **Gouden Bocht** (Golden Bend). Many of these grand old buildings now house banks and financial institutions.

Along the Golden Bend

THE NORTHWEST

The Begijnhof

The northwest section abuts the centre, beginning at **Kalver-straat**, the rather brash, shopping street which cuts the centre of Amsterdam from north to south. In a small square called **Spui** you will find a book market on Friday. Off the north side of the square a narrow alleyway, Gedempte Begijnensloot, leads to the entrance of the **Begijnhof** (www.begijnhofamsterdam.nl; daily 9am–5pm; free), a haven of tranquillity in the centre of the city.

The cluster of buildings around a garden was set aside in 1346 for the benefit of the Beguines, members of a lay Catholic sisterhood. They lived simple lives and in return for their lodgings undertook to care for the sick and educate the poor. Although nothing remains of the 14th-century houses, No. 34 is **Het Houten Huys**, Amsterdam's oldest house, dating from around 1425.

Smoking

Smoking is not allowed in public buildings or on public transport, and only in the Rookzone (Smoking Area) on station platforms. Nor is it allowed in hotels, restaurants, cafés and bars, except in separate enclosed areas in which no food or drinks are served, and in small bars operated only by the owner. Smoking coffee shops are permitted to sell cannabis products but not products containing tobacco.

The Catholic chapel dates from 1671 when it was built in a style designed to disguise its purpose. The spectacular stained-glass windows depict the Miracle of Amsterdam. In the centre of the courtyard is the English Reformed Church, where the Pilgrim Fathers worshipped before setting off to the New World (they came here from England before leaving for America).

The last Beguine died in 1971 and today, although the houses are still offered

Stained-glass windows in the English Reformed Church

only to single women of the Christian faith, the women are not expected to undertake lay work.

Amsterdam's Historical Museum

Behind the Begijnhof is the old **Sint-Luciënklooster** (Convent of St Lucy), which became the city orphanage after the Alteration, although it was open only to well-to-do orphans; the poor had to fend for themselves. It was extended several times, including a wing designed by Hendrick de Keyser, and opened in 1975 as the **Amsterdams Historisch Museum** (www.ahm. nl; Mon–Fri 10am–5pm, Sat–Sun 11am–5pm; charge). Its rooms reveal details of the development of this fascinating city through plans, maps and paintings.

28

The Golden Age is brought to life in rooms 5–12, but there is also an interesting section on 20th- and 21st-century Amsterdam, covering the Nazi occupation, and efforts to protect and preserve the city. Tiny details, such as a relief above the

Rembrandt's ruins

The medieval **Stadhuis** (Town Hall) burnt down in 1652 while the building that is now Koninklijk Paleis was being built to replace it. Rembrandt provided a record of the scene when, curiously, he drew the old building in ruins, rather than the new one rising beside it.

Kalverstraat entrance, asking people to support the upkeep of the orphanage, point to the building's original purpose.

The Dam

Once out of the museum, walk north. Take Kalverstraat or, if you find it a little too busy for comfort, take Rokin, which runs parallel to Kalverstraat to the right. This wide street was once a canal, part of which was drained and filled in to allow better access for modern forms of transport. On the far side of the canal is the elegant Georgian facade of the **Allard Pierson Museum** (www.allardpiersonmuseum.nl; Tue–Fri 10am–5pm, Sat–Sun 1–5pm; charge), the archaeological collection of the University of Amsterdam, which has superb temporary exhibitions. Another couple of minutes will bring you to the **Dam**, the symbolic heart of the city.

Koninklijk Paleis

The Dam is a wide cobbled square dominated by the ornate **Koninklijk Paleis** (Royal Palace; www.koninklijkhuis.nl; hours vary depending on official functions; charge), which was completed in 1655. It was originally built as the Town Hall, facing the landing wharfs along Damrak, which at that time would have been busy with ships. The classical design by Jacob van Campen gives some indication of the confidence of the city in the Golden Age – a statue of Atlas carrying the world on his shoulders sits astride the rear of the building, and in the sumptuous interior, only the best materials were used.

When Louis Bonaparte, brother of Napoleon, became king of Holland in 1806, he demanded a palace suitable for his position and in 1808 requisitioned the Town Hall. He furnished it with the finest pieces of the time and left them all behind only two years later when he was forced out of power. It has remained a royal palace ever since, used for ceremonial occasions only.

Nieuwe Kerk, Nationaal Monument and Waxworks

Beside the palace is the **Nieuwe Kerk** (New Church; www. nieuwekerk.nl; daily 10am–6pm, Thur until 10pm when there are exhibitions, but hours may vary; free when no exhibition), built before the palace, but not the oldest church in the city, hence its name. The church has suffered several fires during the course of its history and was stripped of all its treasures in the Alteration. The pulpit is notable for being extremely ornate for a Protestant place of worship. The church is now used as a cultural centre.

The Dam and the magnificent Koninklijk Paleis

Bicycles for hire, see page 113

Across the Dam is the stark, white **Nationaal Monument** commemorating the role of the Dutch in World War II.

On the Dam's south side stands **Madame Tussauds** (daily 10am–between 4.30 and 8.30pm; charge), with a panorama recreating Amsterdam's Golden Age as well as wax models of celebrities.

Make your way behind the Royal Palace to Raadhuisstraat, which leads to the northern canal ring (Herengracht, Keizersgracht and Prinsengracht). Immediately behind the palace is **Magna Plaza**, built in 1899 as the main post office, although its Gothic architecture was considered far too ornate for a civil service department. Refurbished in 1990, it is now home to the city's premier shopping mall.

Around Raadhuisstraat

Raadhuisstraat is the main thoroughfare to the northwestern canal ring and is busy with trams, buses and cars. It will take you quickly to the main attractions of the area but it is not the prettiest or quietest route. Wandering the smaller alleys and lanes to the north and south is much more fulfilling.

Just off Raadhuisstraat, Herengracht 168, is a superb 17th-century residence. The grey sandstone house was built in neoclassical style by architect Philips Vingboons and sports the city's first neck gable. The red-brick **Bartolotti huis** at Nos 170–2 is an ornate Dutch Renaissance mansion built in

1617 by Hendrick de Keyser and his son Pieter, with illuminated 18th-century ceilings by Jacob de Wit.

Westerkerk

Follow Raadhuisstraat until you reach the **Westerkerk** (Apr–Sept Mon–Sat 11am–3pm; free), set in its own square on the left and overlooking Prinsengracht. This church was designed by Hendrick de Keyser in 1619, one of his last commissions. It is reputed to be the burial place of Rembrandt, but no one knows the exact location of the grave (which may no longer exist). One of his pupils, Gerard de Lairesse, painted the organ panels, added in 1686. In summer you can climb the Westerkerk's tower (Apr–Oct Mon–Sat 10am–5pm; charge), the tallest in the city at 83m (273ft), offering incomparable views. The crown on top is a replica of one presented to the city in 1489 by Maximilian I, Holy Roman Emperor.

The Nationaal Monument

Looking down from the Westerkerk tower

Anne Frank House

Turn left beyond the church to Prinsengracht 263, just an ordinary canal house-cum-office but made famous worldwide by events here in World War II. This is the **Anne Frankhuis** (Anne Frank House; www.annefrank.org; daily July–mid-Sept 9am–10pm, mid-Mar–June 9am–9pm, mid-Sept–mid-Mar 9am–7pm, closed Yom Kippur; charge), where during the Nazi occupation this young girl, her family and a small group of others hid for two years in an attempt to avoid deportation.

Anne wrote a diary that paints a clear and terrifying picture of the life the family lived. It comes to an eerie stop only a few days before the family was betrayed and sent to concentration camps. Of the eight people in hiding, only Anne's father survived – Anne died of typhus only weeks before the war ended – and after the war, in 1947, he published the diary, which became a symbol for the oppression of humankind.

The house, built in 1635, has been left much as it was at the time Anne hid here. It opened as a museum in 1960. The secret rooms upstairs, where the family spent the daylight hours, are stark and bleak. A couple of magazine pin-ups still adorn one wall. The wooden bookcase, which hid the doorway to their refuge, is still in situ, propped open for visitors to climb the few stairs. Downstairs were the offices and warehouses of Mr Frank's business, which were recreated in a multimillion-dollar development opened in 1999. Two adjacent buildings have been acquired and refurbished, adding exhibition and audiovisual space, without compromising No. 263 itself. You can see videos of Anne's story and of Amsterdam under occupation, along with photos and artefacts.

The Anne Frankhuis also acts as an education centre and resource for political and philosophical groups fighting oppression in the present day. The museum is always busy in the afternoon: try to visit in the morning if possible (or in late evening during the extended opening hours in summer).

The Jordaan

Cross Prinsengracht to reach the area of the city known as the **Jordaan**. Built as housing for workers and artisans in the early 17th century, it extends roughly from the far bank of Prinsengracht to Lijnbaansgracht and from Brouwersgracht (Brewers Canal) south to Leidseplein. Many of the streets were named after fragrant flowers but this was not the prettiest or sweetest smelling area of Amsterdam in its heyday. Overcrowding

Anne Frank

was rife and with industries such as fabric-dyeing carried out on the ground floors, it was an unsanitary place to live.

Its name is said to derive from the French word *jardin*, since a large contingent of French Huguenots came to live here to escape political persecution. Today, the Jordaan has been revived and become a fashionable residential location. You'll find many bars, restaurants and boutiques in the area. It's a good place to browse for an unusual souvenir.

Rozengracht, a hectic street, marks a Jordaan dividing line. The section to the north of here, and more particularly above Westerstraat, is a maze of alleys, quiet restaurants and thriving workshops, and retains many of its working-class roots. It has many true Jordaaners – traditionally, those who live close enough to the Westertoren to be able to hear the tinkling of its bells – independent-minded students, crafts- and tradespeople born and bred in the quarter. The section

Video installation at the Stedelijk Museum Bureau Amsterdam

below Rozengracht is more gentrified, with individualistic shops on lovely side streets adjacent to the larger canals, and numerous brown cafés.

Stedelijk Museum Bureau Amsterdam

A point of interest for fans of cutting-edge art is the **Stedelijk Museum Bureau Amsterdam** (www.smba.nl; Tue–Sun 11am–5pm; free), at Rozenstraat 59. This offshoot of the city's modern art museum *(see page 58)* is where the most promising, and occasionally the most peculiar, contemporary art being created in the city gets an airing.

Amsterdamse Bos

The Netherlands suffered economic stagnation during

Saving the Jordaan

In the 1970s, parts of the Jordaan were earmarked for demolition, but thanks to widespread protests, the narrow streets were preserved, complete with period features such as these antique street lamps.

the late 1920s and 1930s, as did the majority of other developed countries. One of the methods used to relieve the problems of unemployment was to organise large government funded community projects, such as the **Amsterdamse Bos** (Amsterdam Wood; www.amsterdamsebos.nl), which created the largest recreation area in the city. The park is on the southern fringes of the city and can be reached by one of a number of buses (Nos 166, 170 or 172).

In 1967, it was enlarged to its present 800 hectares (2,000 acres). The trees and plants are now well established, and the wood has become an important habitat for birds, small mammals and insects, making this an ecological centre as well as a park. It has meadows, woodland and a huge lake for rowing, sailing and hourly rowing-boat hire. It features nature reserves, animal enclosures and a botanical garden. With around 48km (30 miles) of bicycle paths and close to 160km (100 miles) of footpaths, there is room for everybody. The stables at Amsterdamse Bos offer woodland horse rides, a perfect way to clear the city air from your system (contact Amsterdamse Manege; tel: 020-643 1432). There is also an open-air theatre, which holds performances in the summer.

In summer local people enjoy an activity called 'day camping', which means heading for an open space, erecting a tent and spending the day relaxing around it – perhaps with a barbecue. At the end of the day, they take the tent down and head home.

Clogs

Clogs, the native footwear of the Netherlands, are still worn by many people who find them as practical as they ever were. Clogs are traditionally made from poplar or willow – two trees that are commonly planted on the river and *polder* banks because they can soak up as much as 1,000 litres (265 gallons) of water per tree per day, keeping water levels under control. The shoes are carved from freshly felled wood and after being shaped are left to dry and harden.

Clogs are traditionally worn two sizes larger than a person's shoe size, with thick socks to fit loosely to avoid rubbing the skin. Only ceremonial clogs (and those for tourists) are painted; everyday pairs are simple and unadorned. You often see farmers and sailors wearing them. Some road workers and deliverymen also find them more comfortable than standard protective boots.

Clogs make popular souvenirs

EXCURSIONS

There are plenty of places within easy day-trip range of Amsterdam, a selection of which we cover in this chapter. Heading out of the city for a day (or two) will enable you to discover the Netherlands on a different level, whether climbing inside a windmill, walking along an historic canal that inspired the young Rembrandt, or eating pancakes in a pastoral village.

Some of the excursions covered below are served by coach tours (ask for details at the tourist office, *see pages 128*), although you can also find your own way by bus, train, bicycle or rented car.

Villages to the North

To the north of Amsterdam are several small towns that not only provide a contrast to the city landscape, they also take you to the heart of agricultural North Holland.

34
35

Windmills

After the invention of the first sawmill in 1592, more than 1,000 windmills were built in the Zaan region, many to provide power for sawing timber for the Zaan shipyards. Eight mills can be seen at Zaanse Schans today, and a ninth is being rebuilt.

Zaanse Schans

One such village is **Zaanse Schans** (www.zaanseschans.nl), a patch of archetypal Dutch landscape just a few kilometres north of Amsterdam centre, near the town of Zaandam. This is a living museum created in 1960, which has brought together a number of farmhouses, windmills, dairies and barns – agricultural buildings that would have been demolished had they not been relocated here. Zaanse Schans has working mills, cheese-making factories and a clog workshop on a canalside. You are free to explore at your own pace and maybe enjoy a *pannenkoek* (pancake) while you're there.

Broek in Waterland and Monnickendam

Broek in Waterland is a village situated just north of the city environs. A small collection of quaint wooden houses, it is surrounded by canals and streams.

Further north is **Monnickendam**, once a large fishing port on the Zuiderzee which lost its *raison d'être* when the Afsluitdijk was completed in 1932, creating the freshwater lake called the IJsselmeer. The pretty gabled buildings that line the main street were once cottages for fisherfolk, and the small port still plays host to a fleet of ships. Many are now in private hands, or serve as pleasure boats in the summer season. There is also a large, private marina filled with sailing boats that head out on to the open water on any sunny weekend. Walk around the old port to find vestiges of the traditional lifestyle. A few families still fish for eels and process them in small 'factories' along the quayside (although most 'IJsselmeer' eels are are now imported). In summer you can buy them from stalls in the town. There are also some good fish restaurants around the harbour.

Marken

Just 5km (3 miles) beyond Monnickendam is **Marken**, one of the most beautiful villages in the Netherlands and home to a community of Calvinist Dutch whose traditions reach back hundreds of years. Situated on an island, Marken had no vehicle access until 1957, when a causeway was opened, linking the village to the mainland. Today the community welcomes visitors but not their cars, which must be left in a large car park on the outskirts.

A few of the older inhabitants of this close-knit community still wear traditional Dutch costume. You can walk through the village with its pretty painted wooden houses to

Traditional windmills at Zaanse Schans

Volendam village
on the IJsselmeer

the picture-perfect harbour. Stop at the tiny museum on the quayside, which holds an eclectic mix of seafaring and fishing memorabilia.

Between Monnickendam and Marken, the causeway leads into open water that is home to thousands of birds in summer. The native herons, ducks and moorhens see many species of migratory birds that fly north for the summer and return south as winter approaches. Head out on the smooth flat road towards the old lighthouse on a lonely promontory at the far end of Marken island.

Volendam and Edam

North of Marken and Monnickendam is **Volendam**, a Catholic counterpart to Protestant Marken. It is the village most changed by tourism, with cafés and souvenir shops lining the harbour. Volendam is still noted for its fish (there are several good restaurants and herring stands) and for distinctive local dress, especially the women's winged lace caps.

The town of **Edam**, famed for its red- or yellow-rinded cheese, has a pretty **Kaaswaag** (Cheese Weigh House) dating from 1592. Look out for the **Kwakelbrug**, wide enough only for single-file foot traffic. The centre of town has an unusual paved overlock, the **Damsluis**, just below the **Captain's House** (1540). Despite its world renown, Edam is still unspoiled and there are some pretty restaurants where you can enjoy lunch before heading back to the city.

Haarlem

Haarlem, just 19km (12 miles) west of Amsterdam, was the
home of Antwerp-born Frans Hals, father of the Dutch
School of painting. The centre of town is a maze of narrow
streets full of historic buildings, which fall under the shadow of the 15th-century **Sint-Bavokerk** (St Bavo's Church;
Mon–Sat 10am–4pm; charge), an enormous Gothic edifice
– also known as the Grote Kerk (Great Church) – which contains one of the finest organs in Europe. Handel and Mozart
both played the instrument, and you can hear it on summer
Tuesday evenings and Thursday afternoons when free recitals
fill the church with music.

Across Lepelstraat from the
church is the 1603 **Vleeshal**
(meat market).

Traditional boats moored in
Monnickendam

On Groot Heiligland to the
south, the **Frans Hals Museum** (www.franshalsmuse-
um.com; Mon–Sat 10am–
4pm, June–Sept also Sun
10am–7pm; charge) is a
suitable testimony to the
town's most famous son,
who was still painting in his
eighties. The museum was
opened in 1913 at the site
of a home for old men.

On the banks of the River
Spaarne is the **Teylers Museum** (www.teylersmuseum.
eu; Tue–Sat 10am–5pm, Sun
noon–5pm; charge), founded
by silk merchant Pieter
Teyler van der Hulst in 1778

and said to be the Netherlands' oldest public collection. Teyler, having no heir, bequeathed his fortune to the advancement of the arts and sciences, and there is an interesting collection of scientific instruments among other artefacts. The museum has collections ranging from minerals and fossils to medals and coins.

Floral Glory

Every spring, from early April to the end of May, the fields south of Haarlem and Amsterdam erupt in a rainbow of colour, which stretches as far as the eye can see. Dutch tulips attract thousands of visitors for these few weeks of beauty.

Sint-Bavokerk, Haarlem

Another attraction for flower lovers is **Keukenhof** (www.keukenhof.nl; late Mar–late May daily 8am–7.30pm; charge), a 28-hectare (69-acre) showpiece garden near the town of Lisse, that welcomes the public. You'll find a host of spectacular crocus, hyacinth and narcissus blooms along with the tulips. The gardens are planted with stately beech and oak trees, enhanced by pretty windmills that add to the authentic Dutch feel. There is also a restaurant and gift shop where you can buy bulbs, blooms and souvenirs.

In **Aalsmeer** you can visit the vast **Bloemenveiling** (Flower Auction; www.flora

holland.com; Mon–Fri 7.30–
11am: charge) at Legmeer-
dijk. Millions of blooms are
auctioned, then dispatched
around the world within
hours. It's fascinating to
watch the action, as minia-
ture trains carry the flowers
through the auction hall for
the buyers to assess, and a
large electronic bid-taker on
the wall reflects the current
bidding price. The sheer size

Flowers in Keukenhof

of the auction house is what gives pause for thought – the
walkway for spectators is 1.6km (1 mile) long.

Leiden

The rich history and university atmosphere makes **Leiden** ◀ **41**
an interesting place to visit. Just a half-hour by train from
Amsterdam, this medieval city, famous for cloth-making and
brewing industries, joined the Dutch Revolt against Spain
and was besieged. It eventually rallied after the dykes were
broken and the land was flooded, enabling a rescue fleet to
sail directly across the countryside and save the city.

Rembrandt was born in Leiden, as were other Dutch
Masters such as Gerrit Dou, Jan Steen, Gabriel Metsu and
Jan van Gooyen. This is also where the Pilgrim Fathers
formed a community in 1608, seeking refuge from religious persecution in England. Leiden University is probably the most prestigious in the Netherlands, with alumni
including René Descartes and the 17th-century lawyer,
Hugo Grotius.

Visit the **Molen Museum De Valk** (De Valk Windmill Museum; Tue–Sat 10am–5pm, Sun 1–5pm; charge;) on Tweede

Binnenvestgracht, and the **Museum De Lakenhal Leiden** (Tue–Fri 10am–5pm, Sat–Sun noon–5pm; charge) on Oude Singel, with rooms illuminating Leiden's history. The inner city is ringed by two concentric canals, so a stretch of water is never far away, and there are many bridges to cross. Make your way to the marketplace where the old and new branches of the Rhine meet and open markets are held on Wednesday and Saturday. Then cross the bridge to Oude Rijn and turn right towards the **Burcht**, Leiden's 12th-century castle. Have a drink or a meal at the Koetshuis brasserie-restaurant in the courtyard. The **Hortus Botanicus der Rijksuniversiteit** (University Botanical Garden; www.hortus.leiden univ.nl; Apr–Oct daily 10am–6pm, Nov–Mar Tue–Sun 10am–4pm; charge) along Wittesingel are also worth a visit.

Alkmaar

Dutch cheeses are world renowned, and the small red and yellow Edam and Gouda rounds can be found in supermarkets and grocery stores in just about every country of the Western world. However, in the Netherlands, cheese isn't so much an industry as a way of life, and tradition still has a part to play in the production and distribution of the product.

> **Make love not war**
>
> Alkmaar's municipal museum, Stedelijk Museum Alkmaar (Tue–Sun 10am–5pm; charge) on Canadaplein, is housed in a Renaissance guild house. It contains the 16th-century *Siege of Alkmaar*; bizarrely, the painting shows a couple making love while the battle rages.

Alkmaar is a small town 30km (19 miles) north of Amsterdam. It has been the centre of cheese production for many centuries and is now the only town that still has a cheese market, held every Friday morning during the summer. There is also another busy market in town on Friday, selling goods and produce other than cheese.

42

Alkmaar cheese porters

The 14th-century **Waaggebouw** was a chapel before being converted into a weigh house. On Friday the square in front of it becomes a showcase of cheese, when rounds of cheese are piled there waiting to be weighed. Porters, dressed in white trousers, white shirts and coloured hats, transport them on wooden sleds with shoulder harnesses and playfully attempt to be the fastest, much to the amusement of the crowds.

The Waaggebouw contains the **Hollands Kaasmuseum** (Holland Cheese Museum; www.kaasmuseum.nl; Apr–Oct Mon–Thur and Sat 10am–4pm, Fri 9am–4pm; charge).

Nearby, the **Grote Kerk** (Great Church; www.grotekerk-alkmaar.nl; Tue–Sun 10am–5pm; charge) contains the tomb of the count of Holland, Floris V, who granted Amsterdam its rights to carry goods toll-free in the 13th century. In a sense he started the economic life of the city and could be said to be its founding father.

WHAT TO DO

SHOPPING

Amsterdam is a gold mine for those who like to browse. The city has not yet been taken over by the international chain stores, and the narrow streets of the centre, the canal rings and the Jordaan area are home to myriad small, independent boutiques, where you can wander for hours in search of an individual gift. The nearest Amsterdam has to 'international' shopping is Kalverstraat, a street that's home to trendy, if mostly undistinguished, fashion outlets and department stores, and P.C. Hooftstraat, noted for its designer names.

Most museums have good gift shops, especially the Jewish Historical Museum, Maritime Museum , Amsterdam Historical Museum, Rembrandt House Museum, Science Center NEMO and the Nieuwe Kerk. The Rijksmuseum and Van Gogh Museum have a shared shop on Museumplein.

Amsterdammers love to shop for their homes. Although many live in small apartments, what they lack in floor space they make up for in the quality of their environments, and interior design stores feature in every shopping area.

Markets

Amsterdam has a good number of authentic street markets. Some cater to those with a specialist interest and are by no means a place to find inferior or cheap goods. Perhaps the most famous market is the partly floating **Bloemenmarkt** (Flower Market), which is held on the Singel every day. As well as beautiful blooms you can buy bulbs and tubers to take home (if your country's customs authorities allow this).

You will see a lot of bikes and blooms in Amsterdam

The **flea market on Waterlooplein** also has an international reputation. Many stallholders have moved to other locations in the city, although second-hand clothes still feature heavily, along with ethnic wear. It is open every day except Sunday.

A summer **Antiekmarkt** (Antiques Market) meets at Nieuwmarkt on Sunday from May to October. On Elandsgracht and Looiersgracht in the Jordaan is a market for cheaper antiques, collectables and bric-a-brac. The stalls are found inside a number of old houses, which makes it the perfect place to shop on a rainy day. There is a **Boekenmarkt** (Book Market) every Friday on Spui in front of the private entrance to the Begijnhof. Publications in various languages are on sale. The **Kunstmarkt** (Art Market) on Thorbeckeplein takes place on Sunday between March and November. This is a forum for independent artists in all genres. The **Postzegelmarkt** (Stamp Market) on Nieuwezijds Voorburgwal attracts collectors on Wednesday and Saturday afternoons. One of the largest general street markets in Europe is the **Albert Cuypmarkt**, selling everything from fruit and vegetables to textiles from Monday to Saturday.

The Nine Little Streets

The Negen Straatjes (Nine Little Streets) are a number of small alleys that form the ribs linking the Herengracht, Keizersgracht and Prinsengracht canals. Here you will find some individual boutiques with imports from all over the world, as well as antiques shops and designer clothing outlets. It's also a great place for small restaurants and bars.

For designer fashions, visit P.C. Hooftstraat and neighbouring Van Baerlestraat, which border Museumplein. Although this couture quarter is small compared with that of Milan or Paris, you will still find a good range to choose from, and stores stock work by international and Dutch designers.

Inside De Looier, an antiques market in the Jordaan

What to Buy

Antiques. The rich legacy of the Dutch colonial period makes Amsterdam an interesting city for antiques. European period furniture mixes with Southeast Asian artefacts and art – there are dealers in almost every specialist area. This is not a place for amateur collectors. Prices are high but so is quality, the expertise of the dealers, and the advice they give. Many of the finest shops are found around Nieuwe Spiegelstraat and the small streets leading from the Rijksmuseum towards the city centre; there are also a number on Rokin.

There are also many stores selling 'collectables', including early 20th-century light fittings, taps and door furniture.

Art. The lure of the city for creative people has existed for centuries and modern artists follow in the wake of Rembrandt and the Dutch Masters. Dozens of small galleries offer everything from classical to pop art. Exhibitions at the major galleries also promote the work of up-and-coming younger artists as well as

Diamonds are forever

established names. Street art is also very much in evidence, especially in the summer. For a more classic form of art, paintings and prints of windmills or canal houses can be found all across the city.

Diamonds. Before World War II, Amsterdam was a major centre for the buying and polishing of diamonds. The industry deteriorated because of the loss of many Jewish families who ran the major diamond houses, but a slow recovery ensured its survival. Today the industry is known for the quality of its polishing and the expertise of its independent traders.

Three main diamond houses in the city are responsible for buying and polishing the majority of the stones. They sell to smaller dealers but also to the public. You will be able to see diamond polishers at work before you buy. You can choose from loose stones or finished pieces of jewellery. The three are: **Amsterdam Diamond Centre**, Rokin 1–5, at the Dam (tel: 020-624 5787); **Coster Diamonds**, Paulus Potterstraat 2–8, at Museumplein (tel: 020-305 5555); and **Gassan Diamonds**, Nieuwe Uilenburgerstraat; 173–5, and at Oudeschans (tel: 020-622 5333)

Plants. The Netherlands is famed worldwide for its flowers, and particularly the beautiful spring tulip displays in the fields to the west and southwest of Amsterdam. Yet blooms are produced all year in hothouses scattered across the countryside and can be purchased at the Bloemenmarkt on the Singel. In addition to fresh flowers you can also buy bulbs to take home. The streets of Amsterdam have many independent florists with imaginative ideas in fresh and dried flowers. Even if you don't buy, it may well inspire you for your return home.

Cigars. There is a small but high-quality cigar industry in the Netherlands offering a wide choice in terms of size and price. **P.G.C. Hajenius**, Rokin 92–6 (tel: 020-623 7494) have been producing their own brand and importing the best in the world for 170 years. They also have a smoking café if you want to sit and enjoy your cigar on the premises. Their shop, specially built for the company in 1915, has a beautiful Art Deco interior.

Jenever. Only the Dutch and Belgians produce this alcoholic drink, a kind of hybrid of English gin and German *schnapps*. It is often bottled in distinctive stone flagons, which make wonderful souvenirs – and excellent rustic candlesticks when empty (as you can see in the city's many 'brown bars').

Flowers on display at the Bloemenmarkt

Blue and white Delftware

Pewter. You will find old pewter objects in the Amsterdam Historical Museum and the Maritime Museum. In the Golden Age, pewter was used to make everyday utensils such as mugs, plates and kettles. Today, it is fashioned into all kinds of objects, although larger pieces are expensive.

Silver. Modern silver is fashioned into a range of objects and styles of jewellery. You will also find lots of older pieces – some quite exquisite – in the form of spoons, ornate pill and snuff boxes, or letter openers.

Delftware. The pottery style known as Delft (after the city southwest of Amsterdam) was produced across the country during the Golden Age and, in the 1600s, many fine pieces came out of a pottery on Prinsengracht. The blue and white finish is standard Delft, and you will find it at many high-class outlets, with prices to match the quality. For an eclectic selection of old and new Delftware, visit **Galleria d'Arte Rinascimento**, Prinsengracht 170 (tel: 020-622 7509). At **Jorrit Heinen**, with branches at Prinsengracht 440 (tel: 020-627 8299) and Muntplein 12 (tel: 020-623 2271) you can buy examples of the traditional pottery styles, and some fine modern pieces too. The company also has two branches in the Markt in Delft.

Other Dutch souvenirs. You will find a range of souvenirs that epitomise the Holland of tourist brochures. Wooden clogs feature prominently, either plain or painted in bright colours. Windmills are found everywhere, on tea-towels, T-shirts and fridge magnets.

ENTERTAINMENT

It is said that there are more than 40 different performances taking place every evening of the year in Amsterdam, so you will not be at a loss for things to do. Concert halls and theatres are found all across the city with ballet, opera, rock, jazz and classical performances all featured regularly. There are also plenty of venues staging more risqué or avant-garde performances.

The main venues for major performances are the **Concertgebouw** (tel: 0900 671 8345; www.concertgebouw.nl) near to Museumplein, for orchestral and chamber concerts; the **Muziektheater** (tel: 020-625 5455; www.hetmuziektheater.nl) on the banks of the Amstel, which is home to the National Ballet and the Netherlands Opera; and the **Beurs van Berlage** (tel: 020-521 7575; www.beursvanberlage.nl), the beautiful old Stock Exchange building near the Dam, now a twin-hall concert venue and home to the Netherlands Philharmonic Orchestra and the Netherlands Chamber Orchestra.

The city's newest large musical venue is the **Muziekgebouw aan 't IJ** (tel: 020-788 2000; www.muziekgebouw.nl), on the south bank of the IJ waterway, just

Late-night jazz

east of Centraal Station. It stages performances of modern, world and experimental music. In an annexe is the renowned Bimhuis (tel: 020-788 2188; www.bimhuis.nl) jazz and blues club.

The Koninklijk Theater Carré (tel: 0900-252 5255; www.theatercarre.nl), near the Magere Brug on the Amstel, hosts musicals. Boom Chicago (tel: 020-423 0101; www.boomchicago.nl) in Leidseplein is the venue for stand-up comedy in English. Melkweg (tel: 020-531 8181; www.melkweg.nl) on Lijnbaansgracht is an offbeat arts centre-cum-club, with concert hall, disco, experimental plays (some in English) and art exhibitions.

Clubbing in Amsterdam

You can book tickets for performances on arrival but popular acts sell out quickly, so reserve in advance if there is something you particularly wish to see. The easiest way to book tickets in advance is through the Amsterdams Uitburo. They produce a monthly magazine called *Uitkrant* with a listing of major performances (in Dutch, but listings are fairly easy to follow). Contact them on (tel: 020-795 9950; www.amsterdam suitburo.nl; have your credit card ready). Tickets can either be posted to your home address or kept at the AUB office in Leidseplein for you to collect at a later date. When in Amsterdam, pick up their English brochure, *Culture in Amsterdam*, at the AUB's office.

At any given time there will be temporary art exhibitions at galleries and museums around the city. EYE Film Instituut Nederland (tel: 020-589 1400; www.filmmuseum.nl) in Vondelpark (due to move to a shiny new home in Amsterdam–Noord at the end of 2011) holds special showings and film festivals.

The Holland Festival is a programme of art events in June. In Amsterdam, parks and squares are filled with organised activities, and many galleries and concert halls hold events (tel: 020-523 7787: www.hollandfestival.nl).

Cruising the canals is an excellent way of viewing the city. Many bridges and historic buildings are lit at night, and it is possible to have dinner while cruising along. Most of the canal boat tour companies *(see page 121)* offer at least one evening cruise that includes wine and cheese or a full dinner.

Bars and Clubs

Amsterdam bars can be divided into two broad types: the old-fashioned traditional *bruine kroegen* (brown cafés), and contemporary bars and lounges. A small third category, the *proeflokaal* (tasting house), follows the brown-café style. An evergreen brown café is **Hoppe**, Spui 18–20 (tel: 020-420 4420; www.cafe-hoppe.nl), where imbibers spill out onto the pavement in warm weather. In the Jordaan, **'t Smalle**, Egelantiersgracht 12 (tel: 020-623 9617; www.t-smalle.nl), is a popular brown café and tasting house. Head to the redeveloped KNSM Island in the eastern harbour for an even newer café with a traditional patina: **Kanis en Meiland**, Levantkade 127 (tel: 020-418 2439; www.kanisenmeiland.nl). A cool modern spot is **XtraCold Ice Bar**, Amstel 194–6 (tel: 020-320 5700; www.xtracold.com).

There is no shortage of dance clubs and other nightspots, particularly around Leidseplein and Rembrandtplein, but also scattered around the city. The large multipurpose **Melkweg**, Lijnbaansgracht 234a (tel: 020-531 8181; www.melkweg.

nl), just off Leidseplein, is a dance club, bar, cinema, live music venue and theater all in one. On the far side of Vondelpark, the smaller **OCCII**, Amstelveenseweg 134 (tel: 020-671 7778; www.occii.org), is similar, only in a grungier, more cutting-edge vein. A good central dance venue is the **Winston Club**, Warmoesstraat 129 (tel: 020-623 1380; www.winston.nl), on the edge of the Red Light District.

SPORTS

Football
This is an incredibly popular sport in the Netherlands, and Ajax (www.ajax.nl), the Amsterdam team, has been one of the most successful in Europe for decades. Ajax play at the Amsterdam ArenA (www.amsterdamarena.nl), a fine modern stadium used for numerous events. It is almost impossible to get tickets in Amsterdam, but you can buy a travel package on the Ajax website that includes match tickets.

Watersports
With so much water around, it's not surprising that water-based sports are so popular. Even on city-centre canals you will find pedaloes to hire, operated by Canal Bike (tel: 0900-333 4442; www.canal.nl). You can also captain your own boat: Canal Motorboats has a dock at the Zandhoek marina on Realen Island, west of Centraal Station (tel: 020-422 7007; www.canal-motorboats.com). On the wider waterways you will find rowing and sailing clubs that operate in good weather all year round. Out on the freshwater IJsselmeer lake on any sunny weekend you may see hundreds of white and brown sails. Boats can be hired from Monnickendam and other harbour towns, or you can take a trip on a crewed boat; book well in advance (Holland Zeilcharters Monnickendam, 't Prooyen 4a, 1141 VD Monnickendam; tel: 0299-652 351; www.sailing.nl).

Cycling

Cycling for fun as well as for commuting is a major activity. Cycle routes run parallel to most roadways, making longer journeys relatively easy, and sporting groups or families head out to villages such as Monnickendam or Marken. Closer to the centre, a ride through Vondelpark gives you a feeling of being out of the city. If you would like to tour with a group, contact Yellow Bike, Nieuwezijds Kolk 29 (tel: 020-620 6940; www.yellowbike.nl). They organise daily tours with English guides from April to October *(for bike hire, see page 10)*.

Skating

Winter sports have traditionally played a big part in the lives of Amsterdammers. When the rivers and canals freeze, everyone is out on the ice – with long-distance skating through the countryside from town to town on cold, bright Sundays.

Cycling with the kids in tow, Amsterdam-style

EATING OUT

Dutch national cuisine includes a limited range of dishes, yet eating out in Amsterdam can be one of the highlights of the trip. The reason? Many of the more than 100 nationalities that inhabit the city have brought their own unique culinary delights to Amsterdam's restaurants. You could stay in the city for over a month and not eat the same style of food twice. This offers boundless opportunities to try something new, and means you will never get tired of eating out.

Amsterdam is a café society, and restaurants and bars form a lively part of the social scene. Restaurants range from the very formal to the informal, with prices to match.

Brown Cafés

Amsterdam's traditional brown cafés (so-called because walls and ceilings have turned brown from age and smoke) are identified by dark, cosy, wooden interiors. The only audible sound is the buzz of lively conversation and the tinkle of glasses being rinsed. Coffee is generally brewed, not machine-made, and if you fancy a snack to go with your beer or spirit, there is usually a plate of olives or cheese. These cafés define the Dutch word *gezelligheid*, which means a state of cosiness or conviviality. This is where local people come for a few beers after work, to play cards, engage in political debates and tell tall tales.

The more elegant and stylish grand cafés in the city serve lunch and desserts, and tend to have high ceilings, more light, reading tables and a wider variety of music than brown cafés. There are also cafés where you can play chess, throw darts, or play pool or billiards. There are men's cafés, women's cafés and even night cafés, which close around 5am.

Dutch Dishes

Traditional Dutch food is seasonal and based on whatever was harvested from the land or the sea, with light summer dishes and hearty, filling winter foods. Arable farms abound in the countryside, and meat dishes do not generally play a major part in Dutch cuisine. Fish and dairy produce are always considerably more prevalent.

Pancakes are a Dutch favourite

The Dutch breakfast *(ontbijt)* is a hearty one. Slices of ham and cheese, and perhaps boiled eggs with various breads and jam or honey are accompanied by strong milky coffee.

For lunch the Dutch enjoy *pannenkoeken*, pancakes thicker than the French *crêpe* and made fresh as you order them. You can have savoury ones (made with eggs and bacon, for instance) or sweet toppings, with fruit, chocolate and cream, or perhaps even one of each. *Uitsmijter* is another interesting and popular lunch dish, served in Dutch homes and in cafés. It consists of a slice of bread toasted on one side, on to which a slice of ham and a fried egg are added.

Broodjes or sandwiches are available with a vast range of fillings. The local ham and Dutch cheeses are probably the most authentic if you want to eat local, and the combination is delicious eaten hot in a *toastje* or toasted sandwich.

Patates frites (chips, French fries) are served and eaten at any time of day – you will see the vendors' stalls in squares or on street corners. They are thickly cut and served with a spoonful of thick mayonnaise.

You'll find fish on most menus

Winter dishes are warming and hearty. Start with a bowl of *erwtensoep*, a thick pea soup with chunks of sausage. Served with heavy bread or pumpernickel, it constitutes a meal in itself. The other main type of soup is *bruine bonen soep* made with red kidney beans. This may then be followed by *stamppot*, a purée of potatoes and vegetables (usually kale or cabbage) served with slices of *rookworst* (thick smoked sausage), or *hutspot*, made with beef.

Fish

Fish *(vis)* has been a mainstay of the Dutch diet for many generations. Try halibut *(heilbot)*, cod *(kabeljauw)* or haddock *(schelvis)*, all of which come from the North Sea off the Dutch coast. Local oysters *(oesters)* and mussels *(mosselen)* are especially good, and smoked eel *(gerookte paling)* is a Dutch delicacy. A dish that harks back to the Calvinists, and which is light on the palate, is a basic meal of plaice *(schol)* with vegetables, where the fish is grilled and served with butter. You'll also find freshwater fish, called 'sweetwater fish' *(zoetwatervis)* by the Dutch, from some canals and rivers.

Another favourite is herring *(haring)*, a small Atlantic fish that swims close to the North Sea shores. It is eaten raw (you'll see them sold like this at stalls in the street). The typical Dutch way to eat herring is to take the tail in one hand, hold it above your mouth and slowly eat it in bites, so that the herring gradually disappears and only the tail is left. Amsterdammers often prefer herring chopped and served with raw chopped onions.

Cheese

Cheese *(kaas)* is eaten more often at breakfast or lunch rather than with dinner. Several types of cheese from the Netherlands have become internationally famous. Both Gouda and Edam, named after the towns where they are produced, are easily identifiable, being round in shape and covered in red (for export) or yellow wax that keeps the cheese airtight, allowing it to be kept for many months. Traditionally, they were stored in a cool larder and a large cheese could last a family several weeks.

Desserts

The Dutch aren't known for a sweet tooth, although most cafés and restaurants will have *appelgebak* (apple pie) on the menu. You will also find *stroopwafels*, thin round waffles filled with golden syrup and butter; and *poffertjes*, small, shell-shaped pieces of dough, fried until brown in butter and sugar.

Cheese is eaten for breakfast or lunch in the Netherlands

French-inspired
cuisine in Amsterdam

Indonesian Cuisine

The expansion of Dutch interests in the Golden Age brought a wealth of new ingredients and flavourings from the Far East. This added interest to native dishes, such as the Dutch habit of sprinkling nutmeg on cooked vegetables, but also, over the centuries, close ties with what is now Indonesia created a second Dutch national dish – *rijsttafel* (literally translated as 'rice table'). There are numerous Indonesian restaurants throughout the city offering *rijsttafel* with 10, 15 or 20 dishes. If you don't want a full *rijsttafel*, order *nasi rames*, a smaller selection of dishes served with rice – an ideal choice for lunch.

Rijsttafel is a Dutch invention, an interpretation of Indonesian cuisine – though often less spicy than the real thing – which became accepted both in the old colonies and in the Netherlands as a meal in itself. It consists of a number of small spicy meat, fish or vegetable dishes – up to 32 in total – and a communal serving of rice. Take a serving of rice and put it in the middle of your plate, then take small amounts of the spicy dishes and place them around the outside of the rice. The small courses balance one another in taste, texture and heat (spiciness) to excite the palate.

The standard dishes include *babi* (pork), *daging bronkos* (roast meat in coconut milk), *goreng kering* (pimento and fish paste) and small skewers of meat *(satay)* with peanut sauce. Any dish that is labelled *sambal* is guaranteed to be hot (spicy), but hot dishes will be tempered with cooling ones such as marinated fruits and vegetables.

Food of the World

Wander along just a few of Amsterdam's streets and it will soon become apparent that choice is the name of the game when it comes to eating out. If you want the best in French cuisine – and there are a number of restaurants with Michelin stars here – you will not be disappointed. Japanese restaurants abound for the very best in *sushi* or *teppanyaki*. Even good old steak can be found in Argentine, American and Mexican style.

Other European cuisines on offer are found in Spanish tapas bars and Greek tavernas – and you need look only a little further afield to find Egyptian kitchens, Moroccan *couscous* houses and South African bistros. All these are in addition to a fine selection of Italian and Chinese restaurants. Your trip to Amsterdam could well prove to be a culinary journey right around the world.

A cosy restaurant interior

What to Drink

The Dutch love their bars. You'll find one on almost every street corner, warm, welcoming places where you can sit for hours. The staple place to socialise is the *bruine kroeg* (brown café), as much an institution as the pub is in Britain. So called because of their brown-stained walls, low lighting and smoky interiors, brown bars sell alcohol, coffee and light snacks *(see page 96)*.

Traditional Dutch bars have historically centered on two products. Beer is one and *jenever* (pronounced 'yen-eyfer') the other. At one time, distillers and brewers had tasting

The Threatened Coffee Shop Scene

In Amsterdam, so-called 'coffee shops' have sold cannabis under a quasi-legal status for more than three decades. Their presence is tolerated largely because they segregate the users of soft drugs from the dealers who peddle harder substances.

There are around 230 establishments in the city where customers are able to sit back and indulge without suffering the paranoia of the wrong-doer. Ranging from unassuming neighbourhood joints to multi-level coffee shops with internet access, pool tables and TV screens, they are generally easy to spot, often having psychedelic paint schemes or depictions of the marijuana leaf on the outside.

This seemingly idyllic picture for the cannabis puffer might be about to change. The national coalition government elected in 2010 announced its intention to force the country's coffee shops to become private clubs, with membership available only to residents of the Netherlands. This would shut out foreign visitors, including the many 'drugs tourists' who pour into the country from Germany, Belgium, France, Britain and beyond. It is far from certain whether this controversial legislation will get past the various political, social and legal obstacles it faces, but the threat to the cosy coffee shop lifestyle is clear.

houses *(proeflokalen)* for their products where buyers would convene to test the latest brews or compare vintages. Today, there are only a few of these remaining in the city and they always serve a range of other drinks, in addition to their traditional one.

De Drie Fleschjes (The Three Bottles) on Gravenstraat (behind Nieuwe Kerk) is the major *jenever* tasting house in the city, and has changed little in appearance

Traditional brown café

since it was opened in 1650 – although the distillery it used to belong to was converted into a hotel in the 1980s. Here you will be able to try different types of *jenever*. The young *(jonge)* clear *jenever* can be rather harsh to the palate, while the old *(oude)*, aged in wooden casks, which impart a slightly yellow colour, is more mellow. There are also varieties of fruit-flavoured *jenever* to try.

In de Wildeman on Kolksteeg is a tasting house for beers, and its minimalist wood-panelled rooms impart something of the feeling of a religious experience to this drink, which has been so much a part of Amsterdam life since the 13th century. There are more than 50 types of beer available on draught, supplemented by nearly 100 different bottled beers. You will be able to undertake a beer tour of Europe if you have the stamina.

Dutch-produced beer is generally a pils variety, slightly stronger than British lager or American beer. If you order beer by the glass it will usually come in a 33cl (12fl oz) mea-

Double Dutch cheer

sure, served chilled. The two fingers of froth that crown your beer are traditional; they are levelled with the top of the glass with a white plastic spatula.

As well as beer and *jenever*, most bars also serve wine, coffee and soft drinks. Coffee is the lifeblood of Amsterdam. The strong black short serving of fresh brew – and it must be fresh – is sold in cafés and bars all across the city. It always comes with a sweet biscuit. Do specify when you order if you want it with milk or cream *(met melk* or *met room)*. This will arrive in a separate container.

TO HELP YOU ORDER

Could we have a table?	**Heeft u een tafel voor ons?**
I'd like a/an/some...	**Ik zou graag... willen hebben**

aperitif	**een aperitief**	milk	**melk**
beer	**een bier**	mustard	**mosterd**
butter	**boter**	pepper	**peper**
bread	**brood**	potatoes	**aardappels**
coffee	**koffie**		**/aardappelen**
dessert	**een**	rice	**rijst**
	nagerecht	salad	**sla**
fish	**vis**	salt	**zout**
fruit	**fruit**	sandwich	**een**
meat	**vlees**		**boterham**
mineral water	**mineraal**	sugar	**suiker**
	water	wine	**wijn**

MENU READER

aardbeien	strawberries	**kool**	cabbage
ananas	pineapple	**lamsvlees**	lamb
biefstuk	steak	**patates frites**	French fries
bloemkool	cauliflower	**perzik**	peach
citroen	lemon	**pruimen**	plums
ei(eren)	egg(s)	**rundvlees**	beef
forel	trout	**sinaasappel**	orange
frambozen	raspberries	**uien**	onions
gehaktbal	meatball	**uitsmijter**	lunch snack
kaas	cheese		of bread, ham
karbonade	chop		and fried eggs
kersen	cherries	**varkensvlees**	pork
kip	chicken	**verse paling**	fresh eel
kokosnoot	coconut	**vrucht**	fruit
konijn	rabbit	**worst/worstje**	sausage

Out on the town in Amsterdam

PLACES TO EAT

We have used the following symbols to give an idea of the price for a three-course meal for one, including wine, cover and service:

€€€€€ over 75 euros   €€€€ 50–75 euros
€€€ 30–50 euros   €€ 20–30 euros   € below 20 euros

THE CENTRE

Hemelse Modder €€ *Oude Waal 11; tel: 020-624 3203.* A mixture of vegetarian and meat dishes with French and Italian influences is served at this hip place along the canal from the Montelbaanstoren. Tue–Sun 6pm–12.30am.

In de Waag €€ *Nieuwmarkt 4; tel: 020-422 7772.* The atmospheric setting of this bar/restaurant, in the Gothic splendour of the old Weigh House with its huge beams, would be enough to recommend it. The decor echoes this structure with huge tables for feasting. A mixed menu of fusion-style dishes is served. Daily 10am–midnight.

Nam Kee €–€€ *Zeedijk 111–13; tel: 020-624 3470.* This abidingly popular Chinese restaurant off Nieuwmarkt could just about double as Amsterdam's Chinatown all by itself, and it is still the heart of the district. It eschews pretty much anything in the way of decor in favour of authentic, no-frills cuisine from an extensive menu. Daily noon–11pm.

Pier 10 €€€ *De Ruyterkade, Steiger (Pier) 10; tel: 020-427 2310.* This small waterfront gem in a former shipping company office behind Centraal Station serves fine seafood and Continental cuisine, complemented by views of the bustling IJ waterway. Daily noon–3pm and 6.30pm–1am.

Restaurant Vermeer €€€€ *(in the NH Barbizon Palace Hotel) Prins Hendrikkade 59–72; tel: 020-556 4885.* One of the finest restaurants in Amsterdam, in a character-rich hotel facing

Centraal Station. serving a French menu with Dutch and Continental influences. Mon–Fri noon–2.30pm and 6–10pm, Sat 6–10pm.

Wilhelmina-Dok €€€ *Nordwal 1; tel: 020-632 3701.* You need to take a short, free ferry trip from Centraal Station to partake of this waterfront restaurant's wide-ranging continental menu. A fabulous, if often windswept, enclosed terrace affords a perfect viewpoint for observing the maritime comings and goings on the IJ waterway. Daily 11am–midnight.

THE SOUTHEAST

D'Vijff Vlieghen €€€€ *Spuistraat 294–302; tel: 020-530 4060.* Don't let the uninviting name – it means 'The Five Flies' – put you off visiting this restaurant close to Spui, because it's an atmospheric haunt with Old Dutch decor, and New Dutch cuisine, and can rustle up a good range of *jenevers* as well. Daily 6–11pm.

Dynasty €€€ *Reguliersdwarsstraat 30; tel: 020-626 8400.* This place close to Koningsplein offers a tempting choice of Thai, Vietnamese and Chinese dishes all conveniently under one roof. You can choose from the set menus or go à la carte to mix and match your meal from different countries. The colourful dining room has a ceiling covered in parasols. Wed–Mon 5.30–11pm.

Haesje Claes €€€ *Spuistraat 273–5; tel: 020-624 9998.* Close to Spui, this comfortable, old-fashioned restaurant is full of nooks and crannies decorated with Delftware and hanging lamps. There is a wide-ranging menu but traditional Dutch dishes (especially stews) and steaks are the specialities of the house. Daily noon–10pm.

Het Tuynhuys €€€ *Reguliersdwarsstraat 28; tel: 020-627 6603.* Mediterranean cuisine and bistro-style decor, in a former coach house near Koningsplein, with a beautiful courtyard where you can eat out in summer. Mon–Fri noon–2.30pm and 6–10.30pm, Sat–Sun 6–10.30pm.

Bolhoed €€ *Prinsengracht 60–2; tel: 020-626 1803*. With a great position beside the canal – and a tiny waterside terrace in summer – the 'Bowler Hat', housed in a former milliner's shop, adds a great location to a menu that brings zest to vegetarian and (for some dishes) vegan dining. The service is friendly and the soups, salads and inventive main courses add a spicy dimension to healthy eating. Daily noon–11pm.

Christophe' €€€€ *Leliegracht 46; tel: 020-625 0807*. Despite the departure of its founder, this canalside restaurant has continued his tradition of creating fine French cuisine with a modern touch and superior wines. Tue–Sat, 6.30–10.30pm.

De Silveren Spiegel €€€€ *Kattengat 4–6; tel: 020-624 6589*. You won't find a more typically Old Dutch-looking place than this. The menu is an updated interpretation of Dutch cuisine, with French added for respectability. Daily 5.30–10.30pm.

De Vliegende Schotel € *Nieuwe Leliestraat 162–8; tel: 020-625 2041*. The 'Flying Saucer' doesn't quite live up to the speedy implication in its name, but this Jordaan eatery lands some out-of-this-world vegetarian and vegan cuisine. You can dine on a pavement terrace in summer. Daily 4–11.30pm.

Manzano €€€ *Rozengracht 106; tel: 020-624 5752*. Spanish restaurant with a relaxed bistro-style atmosphere, in a historic courtyard Jordaan building. Serves everything from an extensive line-up of tapas to authentic paella. Sun–Thur 5–10.30pm, Fri–Sat 5–11pm.

Pancake Bakery € *Prinsengracht 191; tel: 020-625 1333*. Choose from around 70 different oversized Dutch pancakes, savoury or sweet, in this atmospheric warehouse close to Prinenstraat. Daily noon–9.30pm.

Treasure €€ *Nieuwezijds Voorburgwal 115–17; tel: 020-623 4061*. This popular place close to the Dam serves some of the most authentic Chinese cuisine in the city, with several regional styles on the menu. Dim-sum bar. Daily noon–11pm.

A-Z TRAVEL TIPS

A Summary of Practical Information

A

ACCOMMODATION (see also CAMPING, YOUTH HOSTELS and the list of RECOMMENDED HOTELS starting on page 133)

Amsterdam has a wide range of accommodation of all standards and prices, and in most areas of the city. Hotels are rated from one to five stars. Prices are higher in summer. Service charge is included but the 5 percent city tourist tax may not be, so it is worth checking.

Given the architectural style of the buildings in Amsterdam you will find many of the lower-class hotels have steep, narrow staircases and no lift, so check before booking, if you have problems climbing stairs or have young children. Also many old houses have rooms of varying sizes and varying prices, so check this as well.

The Netherlands Board of Tourism & Conventions (NBTC) offices in the UK, US, Canada and some other countries *(see page 128)* can provide a list of hotels in each class and price bracket. Amsterdam's VVV tourist offices *(see page 128)* can also book accommodation if you arrive without a reservation. This is not advisable during the summer or school holidays (exact dates vary but generally the end of May, the end of October, and Easter and Christmas).

The VVV also offers 'arrangement packages' in alliance with various hotels, comprising accommodation and discount vouchers.

Boarding houses and B&B rooms are also available, but usually not with private facilities (Bed & Breakfast Holland, Bestevaerstraat 3, 1056 HD Amsterdam; tel: 020-615 7527; www.bb-holland.nl).

Amsterdam House acts as an agent for a number of apartments and houseboats that can be rented short- or long-term. They can be contacted at 's-Gravelandseveer 7, 1011 KN AE Amsterdam; tel: 020-626 2577; www.amsterdamhouse.com.

I have a reservation.	**Ik heb een reservering.**
What's the rate per night?	**Hoeveel kost het per nacht?**

AIRPORT

Amsterdam Airport Schiphol (AMS; tel: 0900/0141 from inside
Holland; tel: +31 20-794 0800 from abroad; www.schiphol.nl),
14km (9 miles) southwest of the city centre, is one of the busiest
and most modern airports in Europe. It acts as a gateway to
Europe for airlines from around the world. Its tax-free shopping
centre is considered among the best in the world.

There is a good rail connection from Schiphol Airport to Amsterdam Centraal Station. It runs 24 hours a day although there are
fewer trains at night. The journey takes 20 minutes and costs €3.70.

Every 10–30 minutes from 6am– 9pm a Connexxion Hotel Shuttle bus (tel: 038-339 4741; www.schipholhotelshuttle.nl) leaves the
airport, stopping at many of the major hotels. Tickets (€15) are sold
at the Connexxion counter in the arrivals hall and on the bus. The
bus will also take you back to the airport (return ticket costs €24.50).

B

BICYCLE HIRE *(fietsverhuur)*

Amsterdam is one of the most bicycle-friendly cities in the world,
and cycling is a great way to get around. You can hire bikes at
MacBike, Stationsplein 5 at Centraal Station, Weteringschans 2 at
Leidseplein and Nieuwe Uilenburgerstraat 116 near Waterlooplein;
tel: 020-620 0985; www.macbike.nl; and at Rent-a-Bike Damstraat:
Dwarsstraat 20–2, tel: 020-625 5029; www.bikes.nl. Rates begin at
€10 a day. Yellow Bike runs tours around the city and into the countryside (Nieuwezijds Kolk 29, tel: 020-620 6940; www.yellowbike.nl).

Riding a bike in a busy city is potentially risky. Take extra care and
watch out for other road users. It is advisable to wear a crash helmet,
though most Amsterdammers don't. Make sure you are fully insured.

I'd like to hire a bicycle.   **Ik zou graag een fiets huren.**

BUDGETING FOR YOUR TRIP

Flights to Amsterdam: from UK, schedule return flights average £125 plus tax; from New York, specials start at $350 plus tax.

Accommodation: medium-quality double room for one night, €120–80.

Three-course dinner for one excluding drinks: €30–40.

Transport passes: day-pass €7.50, two-day pass €11.50, three-day €15.00 (valid on all forms of public transport).

Entrance to museums: €5–13

Canal cruise: one-hour €10; **dinner cruise:** from €60.

C

CAMPING

There are a number of campsites within a few minutes' travel of the city centre. They are well run and open all ummer although they can fill up early, so it is sensible to make a reservation. Camping Het Amsterdamse Bos is in the large park area to the south of the city with a direct bus link to Centraal Station; tel: 020-641 6868; www.campingamsterdamsebos.nl. Camping Vliegenbos is north across the IJ waterway in 25 hectares (60 acres) of woods; tel: 020-636 8855; www.vliegenbos.com.

CAR HIRE

Amsterdam is a compact city with exceptionally good public transport and roads that favour bicycles. Parking is expensive and difficult to find. Cars found along central canalsides and streets are wheel clamped automatically if they are parked illegally, or if the meter time has expired, and may be towed away. If you are planning to stay in the city, it is unlikely to be worth enting a car, but for touring the countryside it would certainly be worthwhile.

Most of the major international firms are represented in Amsterdam, and you will also find agencies at Schiphol airport.

Avis tel: 0900-235 2847: www.avis.nl
Budget tel: 0900-1576: www.budget.nl
Europcar tel: 0900-0540; www.europcar.nl
Hertz tel: 020-201 3512: www.hertz.nl
Sixt tel: 023-569 865; www.sixtz.nl

Drivers must be over 21 (23 for some agencies) and have held a full licence for at least 12 months. National or international licences must be shown at the time of renting. Collision damage waiver is available at extra cost but is well worth the peace of mind – but do check your own vehicle, household or credit-card insurance, as you may already be covered. Prices start from around €50 per day for a compact car; a five-door hatchback from €80 per day. Prices rise in peak season and drop if you hire the car for more than a couple of days.

| I'd like to hire a car today/tomorrow for one day/a week Please include full insurance. | **Ik zou graag een auto willen huren vandaag/morgen voor één dag/één week Met een all-risk verzekering, alstublieft.** |

CLIMATE

The Netherlands has unpredictable weather patterns similar to those of Britain, characterised by cold, wet winters and warm, wet summers. You can, however, have wonderful sunny days at any time of year, and Amsterdammers always hope for long periods of bright, cold winter spells, but this has not happened often in recent years.

Figures shown below are averages for each month and can vary.

	J	F	M	A	M	J	J	A	S	O	N	D
°C	7	8	11	13	16	18	20	21	17	14	11	8
°F	45	46	52	55	61	64	68	70	63	57	52	46

CLOTHING

It's a good idea to take several different types of clothing, even if you are travelling in summer, when in theory it should be warm. A layering system is the best approach. Always take a rainproof outer layer, whenever you visit, and an umbrella. In winter, a thick coat or jacket will keep you warm in cold spells, when the wind can bite.

On warm summer days, shorts, T-shirts, light shirts and trousers or light dresses are ideal, but always carry an extra layer just in case, and take a light sweater or jacket for the evenings. Comfortable walking shoes are essential, whatever time of year you travel.

Amsterdam is famous for being a casual city, but if you intend to eat at some of the finer restaurants, or visit the ballet or opera, a shirt and tie for men and 'dressy' ensemble for women is appropriate.

CRIME AND SAFETY (see also EMERGENCIES and POLICE)

Statistically, Amsterdam is one of the safest cities in Europe yet certain types of crime persist, notably luggage theft and pickpocketing. Always keep a watch on your luggage, especially at the airport, Centraal Station, or going to and from your hotel. Never carry cash, credit cards or passports in back pockets or an open handbag. Carry them in a body belt or inside a pocket with a zip. Be especially watchful in crowded squares and in the Red Light District.

Do not leave anything in a car, even in the glove compartment or boot; leave the glove box open to show thieves there is nothing inside. If you do have anything stolen, report it immediately to the police.

As far as personal safety is concerned, after dark keep to well-lit major thoroughfares. Many Amsterdammers walk (or go by bicycle) to social engagements, so unless you are very late you will be walking on streets with other people. If in doubt, get a tram – they run until just before midnight, and there will probably be a stop near your hotel. Otherwise, take a taxi.

A word on drugs: despite a relaxed attitude to (officially illegal, but tolerated) soft drugs, the possession of hard drugs is a criminal offence.

D

DRIVING

Vehicles are driven on the right in the Netherlands. At roundabouts, give way to traffic from the right (unless signs indicate otherwise).

Road conditions are generally good. Within Amsterdam itself the main thoroughfares are wide and in good condition. Canalside roads are narrow and generally open to traffic travelling in one direction (ie, up one side of the canal and down the other side). This adds to the difficulty of navigating. Just remember to keep the canal to your left and you can be sure that you are travelling on the correct side of the road.

Speed limits. In towns or built up areas: 30 or 50km/h (20 or 30mph). On dual carriageways and motorways: 120km/h (75mph) reduced to 100km/h (62mph) in wet weather. Other limits mays be posted.

Amsterdam has unique factors that drivers need to keep in mind. Cyclists have their own traffic signals and cycle paths, but are still prone to ride without proper care and attention. Some cyclists don't even use lights at night. Trams have priority over all other forms of transport, so watch out for them; they also have their own signals on major roads. Tram tracks become very slippery when wet, so increase your stopping distances as necessary.

Many canalside roads have blind exits (they may be in dips, for instance). Both cyclists and car drivers can pull out without warning. Vehicles meeting on narrow canal bridges can cause problems. Road signs with arrows showing directional priority should be posted; if not, use good humour and common sense – and be prepared to reverse off the bridge to allow traffic to flow. Canalside roads and many other thoroughfares in the old part of the city can only accommodate one vehicle. This means that when delivery and rubbish lorries make their stops, vehicles behind them can be held up for many minutes.

If you travel to Amsterdam in your own car, you will need to carry your driving licence, registration document, or document of ownership, valid insurance, a red warning triangle in case of breakdown, and

US: Museumplein 19; tel: 020-575 5300; http://amsterdam.usconsulate.gov.

EMERGENCIES *(see also POLICE)*

For emergencies (fire, police or ambulance) dial 112.

If you have a problem with theft or pickpocketing, there is a large police station at Lijnbaansgracht 219; tel: 0900 88443; www.politie-amsterdam-amstelland.nl.

G

GAY AND LESBIAN TRAVELLERS

Amsterdam is an extremely friendly city for gay and lesbian visitors. There are hotels that cater specifically for them and a vibrant social scene. There is a gay and lesbian community centre: COC, Rozenstraat 14; tel: 020-626 3087; www.cocamsterdam.nl. The Gay and Lesbian Switchboard also has information about what's happening in the city (tel: 020-623 6565; www.switchboard.nl).

GETTING THERE

By air. Most of the world's major airlines operate flights to Amsterdam Airport Schiphol, and KLM (www.klm.com), the national airline of the Netherlands, has a large network and flies from the UK, US, Canada, South Africa, Australia and New Zealand. For reservations contact KLM in Holland on tel: 020-474 7747, in the UK tel: 0871-231 0000, or toll-free in the USA on 800-225 2525.

There are several flights to Schiphol daily from London airports, Manchester and other regional UK airports. Flights from London take around one hour. British Airways (tel: 0844-493 0787; www.ba.com), BMI (tel: 0844-848 4888; www.flybmi.com), easy-Jet (www.easyjet.com) and KLM all operate services. Aer Lingus (tel: 0818-365000; www.aerlingus.com) has regular service to Amsterdam from Dublin.

Other airlines that run nonstop services to Schiphol include Delta (www.delta.com), Continental (www.continental.com) and United (www.united.com)

By sea. P&O Ferries operates a daily service from Hull to Rotterdam (tel: 0871-664 2121; www.poferries.com). Stena Line (tel: 08447-170 7070; www.stenaline.co.uk) sails from Harwich to Hoek van Holland. DFDS Seaways (tel: 0871-522 9955; www.dfdsseaways.co.uk) from Newcastle to IJmuiden (tel: 0871-522 9955; www.dfdsseaways.co.uk).

By rail. Travellers from Britain can use the Eurostar service (tel: 08432-186 186; www.eurostar.com) from London through the Channel Tunnel to Brussels, and onward from there by high-speed Thalys train. For those who wish to visit Amsterdam as part of a European rail tour, there are special prices for monthly passes and special ticket prices for under-26s and over-65s. Further details can be found on the website www.eurorail.com.

By road. Eurolines (tel: 0871-781 8181; www.eurolines.com) run up to five buses a day from London to Amsterdam . By car, you can either take one of the car ferry services above, or ferries that sail to ports in Belgium and France; or put your car on a Eurotunnel shuttle train (tel: 08443 353 535; www.eurotunnel.com).

GUIDES AND TOURS

There are a number of qualified English-speaking guides who offer tours of the city. Some have specialities, some take groups or offer an individual service. Contact the VVV *(see page 128)* for a list.

A number of companies offer boat tours along the canals and these are probably the most popular activities in the city. Multilingual commentary keeps you informed about the attractions as you float along past them. Contact Rederij Lovers (tel: 020-530 5412; www.lovers.nl) or simply head to Damrak and Stationsplein and other docks from where the boats depart.

Yellow Bike offers accompanied bike tours of the city with English-speaking guides (tel: 020-620 6940; www. yellowbike.nl).

H

HEALTH AND MEDICAL CARE

The Netherlands is a modern, well-run country, and its medical facilities are excellent There are no health concerns, although mosquitoes can be a nuisance in the summer, so anti-mosquito sprays or creams are useful. You will not need inoculations and the water is safe to drink. Most doctors and other medical professionals speak English. Always take out suitable travel insurance to cover any health problem you may have on your trip. You will be asked to pay for some medical treatment and should cover yourself against something serious happening to you. If you are an EU citizen, you will be covered for medical treatment by participating doctors/hospitals if you have a European Health Insurance Card (EHIC), available online at www.ehic.org.uk. You will need to pay for treatment at the time but will be able to claim a refund on return.

Many proprietary brands of drugs are available over the counter from any pharmacy (*apotheek*). A trained pharmacist will be able to give sound advice about medicines for minor ailments. Call 592 3434 to find out which pharmacies are open after hours and for referral to local doctors and dentists.

L

LANGUAGE

There are around 30 million speakers of Dutch in the world, with Afrikaans (South Africa) and Flemish (Vlaams) of Belgium being closely allied to it. Its structure is similar to German, but it is grammatically simpler. That said, the Dutch usually speak English very well (and other languages passably), so you will rarely need to resort to your language phrasebook. However, knowing and using a few words of the language of the country you are visiting is only polite, and it may gain you some friendly comments.

Do you speak English?	**Spreekt u Engels?**
What does this mean?	**Wat betekent dit?**
I don't understand	**Ik begrijp het niet**
Good morning	**Goede morgen**
Good afternoon	**Goede middag**
Good evening	**Goeden avond**
Please/Thank you	**Alstublieft/Dank u**
You're welcome	**Alstublieft/Graag gedaan**

M

MAPS

The Tourist Office or VVV *(see page 128)* produces several different maps, which may be of use to travellers.

The Tourist Guide to Public Transport in Amsterdam has a map with public transport services superimposed on the basic city map. There is also the *City Map Amsterdam* – a simple map showing the location of all the major attractions. For a very comprehensive map, Michelin's Amsterdam 1cm:150m map covers both the city centre and suburbs, with the city centre expanded for ease of use.

The *Insight Fleximap to Amsterdam* is detailed and easy to use, with a full street index and a laminated finish that means the frequent Amsterdam rain is not a problem.

MEDIA

Newspapers and magazines *(kranten, tijdschriften)*. Many English newspapers and magazines can be readily bought in the city. British daily papers are available soon after they are on sale at home. US papers will be a day old but the *International Herald Tribune* is published daily in Paris, so is on sale on the same day it is published. Most major hotels have a supply in their gift shops or at reception.

TV and radio *(televisie, radio)*. There are a number of Dutch television stations mainly serving the local community and sometimes taking services from various European countries (including British stations). The Dutch use subtitles to translate foreign programmes, rather than dubbing, so you will be able to understand the broadcasts – this is one of the reasons why the Dutch are so adept at speaking English and other languages. Most major hotels offer CNN and the BBC in your room.

In most places in the Netherlands you should be able to get a good reception for BBC radio transmissions.

MONEY

In common with most other EU countries, the euro (€) is used in the Netherlands. Notes are denominated in 5, 10, 20, 50, 100, 200 and 500 euros; coins in 1 and 2 euros and 1, 2, 5, 10, 20 and 50 cents.

Currency can be exchanged in banks and bureaux de change offices that can be found at Centraal Station, in Leidseplein and in major shopping areas. These offices are open longer hours than banks. The GWK Travelex exchange office in Centraal Station provides a good service. Exchange rates and commission fees will be posted in the windows. Traveller's cheques are accepted for commercial transactions and exchanged in the above establishments. You will need your passport to cash or use traveller's cheques.

International ATMs are common and are indicated by the Cirrus or Plus signs on the machine. These machines also provide cash against MasterCard, Visa and other credit and charge cards.

I'd like to change some pounds/dollars.	**Ik wil graag ponden/dollars wisselen.**
Do you accept traveller's cheques?	**Accepteert u reischeques?**
Can I pay with credit card?	**Kan ik met deze credit card betalen?**

Major credit cards are widely accepted in hotels, restaurants and shops, although there may be a minimum limit on payments in shops.

O

OPENING TIMES (see also HOLIDAYS)

Offices and most government offices are generally open Mon–Fri 9am–5pm. Banks are open Mon–Fri 9am–4pm, extended to 5pm for main branches; late opening Thur from 4.30pm–7pm.

Shops are generally open Mon 10am–6pm, Tue–Sat 9am–6pm, (until 9pm on Thur). Some shops open Sun noon–5pm. Many shops extend their opening hours in summer.

P

POLICE (see also EMERGENCIES)

The police headquarters (hoofdbureau van de politie) is at Elands-gracht 117; tel: 0900 8844; www.politie-amsterdam-amstelland.nl. There is also a large police station at Lijnbaansgracht 219; tel: 0900 8844. The emergency number is 112.

Police stations can be found in the following central locations:
• Nieuwezijds Voorburgwal 104 (in the Red Light District)
• Nieuwmarkt (near Waag)
• Prinsengracht 1109.

Police patrols are conducted in cars (with politie painted on the side) and on foot. Police wear navy-blue uniforms and carry firearms. They are approachable to answer basic questions such as giving directions.

POST OFFICES

Post offices are distinguished by the TNT Post (www.tntpost.nl) signs outside. They sell stamps, and change currency and traveller's cheques. The central post office is at Singel 250 and is open Mon–Fri

9am–6pm, Sat 10am–1.30pm. It is often busy, so avoid it if you only want to buy stamps, which are available at the majority of shops selling postcards.

A stamp for this letter/ postcard, please	**Een postzegel voor deze brief/ briefkaart, alstublieft**
airmail	**luchtpost**
registered	**aangetekend**

PUBLIC HOLIDAYS

The following dates are official holidays:

1 January	*Nieuwjaar*	New Year's Day
30 April	*Koninginnedag*	Queen's Birthday
25–26 December	*Kerst*	Christmas

Moveable holidays are as follows:

Goede Vrijdag	Good Friday
Tweede Paasdag	Easter Monday
Hemelvaartsdag	Ascension Day
Tweede Pinksterdag	Whit Monday

All shops and offices are closed for all the above holidays.

T

TELEPHONES

The international code for the Netherlands is 31, and the city code for Amsterdam is 020. To call a number within the city use just the seven-digit number. To call an Amsterdam number from other parts of the Netherlands, dial 020 first. If dialling from outside the country dial your international country code + 31 20 and the seven-digit number.

There are numerous public phones around the city – most obviously outside Centraal Station and in the major squares – which take all major credit and charge cards. Phonecards, available for €5, €10, €20 and €50, can be bought from newsagents and tobacconists.

Roaming is possible on Holland's tri-band and quad-band enabled GSM mobile-phone network. Phones to rent and purchase are widely available from phone stores, as are prepaid SIM cards for using your own (unlocked) phone at Dutch rates. Be sure to bring an appropriate plug adaptor and, if needed, a voltage transformer for charging your phone.

TIME ZONES

The Netherlands is one hour ahead of Greenwich Mean Time (GMT). From the last weekend in March to the last weekend in October, the clocks are advanced one hour – this change corresponds with the rest of the EU. During the European summer, the time differences are:

New York	London	**Amsterdam**	Jo'burg	Sydney	Auckland
6am	11am	**noon**	noon	8pm	10pm

TIPPING

Service charges are included in all bar, restaurant and hotel bills. However, an extra tip to show gratitude for good service is always appreciated. It is appropriate to leave the small change on the table in bars and cafés.

The following situations are still discretionary:

Taxi fares: round up the fare.

Hotel porter: €1–2 per bag.

Maid: €10 per week.

Lavatory attendant: €0.50 – although you may often have to pay this as an entry fee.

Tour guide: 10–15 percent.

Concierge: discretionary according to services provided.

TOILETS

There are few public toilet facilities in the city and the more or less open-to-view urinals – for men only – are pretty grim. However, department stores and the Magna Plaza mall have toilets, and many of the city's top hotels have toilets just off the lobby; there is often a €0.50 service charge for their use. Bars and cafés are designated public places, but it is considered polite to have a drink if you use their facilities. Toilets for females may be indicated with the word *Dames*, and those for males with *Heren*.

| Where is the toilet? | **Waar is het toilet?** |

TOURIST INFORMATION

For information before you depart, contact the Netherlands Board of Tourism & Conventions (NBTC) at the following addresses:

Head office: Nederlands Bureau voor Toerisme & Congressen, Postbus 458, 2260 MG Leidschendam, the Netherlands; tel: (+31 70) 370 5705; www.holland.com
UK and Ireland: PO Box 30783, London WC2B 6DH; tel: 020-7539 7950; e-mail: info-uk@holland.com; www.holland.com/uk.
US and Canada: 215 Park Avenue South, Suite 2005, NY 10003 New York; tel: (212) 370 7360; email: information@holland.com; www.holland.com/us.

In Amsterdam

For information, maps, hotel bookings and tickets, visit one of the VVV tourist offices operated by the Amsterdam Tourism & Convention Board (tel: 020-201 8800; www.iamsterdam.com). Note that there is a small charge for many of their leaflets and maps. The main office is at Stationsplein 10, opposite the entrance to Centraal Station, Mon–Sat 9am–6pm, Sun and holidays 9am–5pm.

In addition, there are several agency offices of the VVV around the city, at commercial and cultural locations.

There is also a Holland Tourist Information bureau in Schiphol Airport, which is useful if you have not booked accommodation.

TRANSPORT

Public transport in Amsterdam is excellent. The GVB (tel: 0900-9292; www.gvb.nl) municipal transport company runs a comprehensive system throughout the day, and a limited bus service through the night. You can use tickets or cards on buses, trams and metro services. Information, route maps, timetables and public transport passes are available from the GVB Tickets & Info office on Stationsplein, outside Centraal Station.

OV-chipkaart. In Amsterdam and throughout the Netherlands, a new travel card, the credit card-size OV-chipkaart has gradually been introduced – 'OV' stands for Openbaar Vervoer (public transport). Three types of OV-chipkaart are available: personal, anonymous and throwaway. Although the personal card offers advantages to residents and long-stay visitors, short-term visitors will find the anonymous and throwaway cards simpler to acquire (although the throwaway card costs more per journey than the other two).

The personal and anonymous cards, both valid for five years, cost €7.50 and can be loaded and re-loaded with up to €30; the throwaway card costs €2.50. Electronic readers automatically deduct the correct fare as you travel. Reduced-rate cards are available for seniors and children. The cards are valid nationwide.

Travel passes. These provide one of the most affordable ways of travelling by public transport. Your pass allows you to travel on any form of public transport at any time for the duration of the pass. Day passes for adults cost €7, but for more days it becomes even better value. A two-day pass costs €11.50, a three-day pass €15.50, a four-day pass €19.50, a five-day pass €24, a six-day pass €27.50 and a seven-day pass €30.

prehensive website, with lots of travel information and news on the city's attractions.

www.noord-holland-tourist.nl The North Holland province tourist office website has information about Amsterdam and in particular about the surrounding areas.

www.visitholland.com The Netherlands tourist office, with information about the whole country and standard tourist information.

www.amsterdamhotspots.nl As its name suggests, this covers the hottest places for eating, drinking, dancing and much more.

www.underwateramsterdam.com Quirky yet insightful guide to what's on and where, dining, events and more.

www.iens.nl Comprehensive dining out website, with reader reviews in both English and Dutch.

www.amsterdam.nl The city government's all-encompassing website is in Dutch only, but may still be worth skimming, and there are links to relevant parts of the tourist office's English website.

Many city hotels, along with some cafés, bars, coffee houses and other locations offer free or paid-for Wi-fi internet access. This has made the dedicated cybercafé virtually superfluous. You are now most likely to find a café or bar that has just a few computers for the use of its patrons.

Y

YOUTH HOSTELS

There are a number of youth hostels in the city. For more information, contact the Dutch youth hostel association, Stayokay, Postbus 92076, 1090 AB, 1018 HA Amsterdam; tel: 020-551 3155; www.stayokay.com. Stayokay hostels offer discounts to members of the International Youth Hostel Association. Amsterdam's main one, Stayokay Amsterdam Vondelpark, with 540 beds, is at Vondelpark (Zandpad 5; tel: 020-589 8996; www.stayokay.com). Reservations are recommended at peak times.

Recommended Hotels

The Netherlands Board of Tourism has rated more than 200 recommended hotels in the city, but there are also many unclassified boarding houses, which represent good value.

Prices are high by international standards but quality is usually high too. The list below recommends hotels in locations around the city and in all classes. It features hotels with a particular character, location or facility that makes them stand out. They all accept major credit cards.

To make a phone enquiry or book from abroad, dial 00 and the country code 31 and delete the first zero from the numbers given here.

The following price categories are for one night for two people in a double room with private facilities. Most large hotels charge 5 percent city tax in addition to the room price; smaller hotels may include the tax in the price. Most hotels include breakfast in the price, although some four- and five-star hotels charge for breakfast separately.

€€€€€	over 350 euros
€€€€	250–350 euros
€€€	160–250 euros
€€	80–160 euros
€	below 80 euros

THE CENTRE

Mövenpick Hotel Amsterdam City Centre €€€€ *Piet Heinkade 11, 1019 BR Amsterdam; tel: 020-519 1200; www.moevenpick-hotels.com.* What you see is clearly what you get at this huge, high-rise modern hotel, overlooking the IJ waterway just east of Centraal Station – the most stunning harbour views in Amsterdam, and all the tried-and-tested virtues of a stellar branch of the Swiss chain.

NH Barbizon Palace €€€€ *Prins Hendrikkade 59–72, 1012 AD Amsterdam; tel: 020-556 4564; www.nh-hotels.com.* A large five-star hotel, next to the Sint-Nicolaaskerk and opposite Centraal Station,

Best Western Apollo Museumhotel Amsterdam City Centre
€€€ *P.C. Hooftstraat 2, 1071 BX Amsterdam; tel: 020-662 1402; www.bestwestern.com.* Just off Museumplein and Leidseplein, this good-value option for independent travellers has modern and comfortable, if not particularly distinguished, rooms, but scores highly for location.

Eden Amsterdam American €€€€ *Leidsekade 97, 1017 PN Amsterdam; tel: 020-556 3000; www.edenamsterdamamericanhotel.com.* Set amid the bars, restaurants and clubs of Leidseplein, the Art Deco American is a hotel favoured by celebrities and pop stars, and is a designated historic monument. The sound proofing does a great job of cutting off the considerable noise that emanates after dark from the many bars and cafés nearby, and sometimes keeps going way into the night.

King's Villa €€€ *Koningslaan 64, 1075 AG Amsterdam; tel: 020-673 7223; www.kingsvillahotel.nl.* Two Edwardian houses set in ample gardens now converted into a stylish hotel on the south side of Vondelpark.

Mozart €€–€€€ *Prinsengracht 518–20, 1017 KJ Amsterdam; tel: 020-620 9546; www.hotelmozart.nl.* Close to Leidseplein, the Mozart is a modest but stalwart canal house hotel, squeezing decent modern furnishings and a few neat design touches into an old building's tight quarters, while regularly updating and striving to provide value for money.

Museum Square €€€ *De Lairessestraat 7, 1071 NR; tel: 020-671 9596; www.museumsquarehotel.nl.* A small hotel opposite the Concertgebouw, a couple of minutes from Museumplein. The rooms are modern and clean.

Nicolaas Witsen €€ *Nicolaas Witsenstraat 4, 1017 ZH Amsterdam; tel: 020-623 6143; www.hotelnicolaas witsen.nl.* On a side street around 15 minutes' walk from the city centre and five minutes south of Museumplein. This is a good hotel for its category, and serves ample breakfasts.

Park Hotel €€€€ *Stadhouderskade 25, 1071 ZD Amsterdam; tel: 020-671 1222; www.parkhotel.nl.* Across the street from Leidseplein and only minutes from Museumplein, the Park has a bar and a restaurant serving Dutch cuisine.

Sandton Hotel De Filosoof €€ *Anna van den Vondelstraat 6, 1056 GZ Amsterdam; tel: 020-683 3013; www.sandton.eu.* On the north side of Vondelpark, a little way out of town, this unusual hotel attracts many like-minded guests. Rooms are named after famous philosophers and are individually designed. There is a bar/lounge and library and an attractive garden, but no restaurant.

Wyndham Apollo Amsterdam €€€€ *Apollolaan 2, 1077 BA Amsterdam; tel: 020-673 5922; www.apollohotelresorts.com.* In Amsterdam South, this five-star hotel is a good base for those who want to be away from the hubbub of the city centre. It stands at a wide canal basin, and has waterside terraces and a marina.

THE NORTHWEST

Ambassade €€€ *Herengracht 341, 1016 AZ Amsterdam; tel: 020-555 0222; www.ambassade-hotel.nl.* Ten historic canal houses within a few minutes' walk of the city centre have been amalgamated to create the Ambassade. The rooms are nicely furnished, but it has no restaurant.

Belga € *Hartenstraat 8, 1016 CB Amsterdam; tel: 020-624 9080; www.hotelbelga.nl.* In the heart of the old town, the Belga is a good budget option for those who want to be in the centre of town. Not all rooms have en suite facilities, so do ask when you make your booking.

Best Western Dam Square Inn €€€ *Gravenstraat 12–16, 1012 NM Amsterdam; tel: 020-623 3716; www.bestwesterndam square.com.* Housed in the building of an old distillery, this cosy hotel has a thoroughly modern interior. It is pleasant, quiet and friendly, and only minutes from the centre.